Mastering Corporate Finance Essentials

Mastering Corporate Finance Essentials

The Critical Quantitative Methods and Tools in Finance

STUART A. McCRARY

WILEY

John Wiley & Sons, Inc.

Published by John Wiley & Sons, Inc., Hoboken, New Jersey.
Published simultaneously in Canada.

For general information on our other products and services or for technical support, please contact our Customer Care Department within the United States at (800) 762-2974, outside the United States at (317) 572-3993 or fax (317) 572-4002.

Wiley also publishes its books in a variety of electronic formats. Some content that appears in print may not be available in electronic books. For more information about Wiley products, visit our web site at www.wiley.com.

Library of Congress Cataloging-in-Publication Data:

McCrary, Stuart A.
  Mastering corporate finance essentials : the critical quantitative methods and tools in finance / Stuart A. McCrary.
     p. cm.—(Wiley finance series)
  Includes index.
  ISBN 978-0-470-39333-8 (cloth)
 1. Corporations—Finance. 2. Business enterprises—Finance. 3. Capital budget.
4. Capital investments. I. Title.
  HG4026.M384 2010
  658.15—dc22

                                                                      2009033769

Printed in the United States of America

10 9 8 7 6 5 4 3 2 1

To my loving wife, Nancy

Contents

Preface

Mastering Corporate Finance Essentials is directed to corporate managers who work with their companies' finance departments and need to understand their work, priorities, and methods. Since corporate finance is at the heart of many key issues, from performance evaluation to project funding, corporate managers must be able to discuss, assess, and contribute to the financial decision-making process to be successful.

The book is written as a text for an executive masters program in business school or as part of the business curriculum in a professional degree program (engineering, law, medicine, etc.). To respect the scarce time of the student, the most important material occupies the main text. Numerous stand-alone inserts, mostly in the detailed answers to review questions, dig into topics more deeply and may present some topics that are more quantitative. Although this text is designed as a concise book covering just the essentials, these inserts devote considerable attention to "quantitative finance," including alternatives to discounted cash flow analysis.

The text is designed to permit the reader to quickly learn present value techniques in Chapter 1. Chapter 2 includes a review of statistics used in corporate finance. Chapter 3 summarizes the most important lessons in corporate finance. Chapter 4 synthesizes material in each earlier chapter to apply it to valuing projects and making investment decisions. Chapter 5 introduces additional tools to evaluate risk. Finally, Chapter 6 extends traditional financial tools to value risk and opportunities.

Each chapter builds a foundation for later chapters. The book ends with important topics in quantitative finance. However, readers can focus on traditional corporate finance and skip the later chapters.

Review questions follow each chapter. The book includes detailed answers to review questions that explore topics in greater depth. A short course can focus on the essential topics presented in the chapters. Instructors with more time can include the questions and answers to present practical, hands-on details. The detailed questions and answers work well for self-study.

This book is quantitative, because the field of finance is quantitative. Difficult topics are explained in clear and simple language. Numerous examples demonstrate how to perform each analysis and assist the reader to understand the material. The text also offers advice on how to use Excel for financial analysis.

A companion text on financial accounting, called *Mastering Financial Accounting Essentials*, presents key accounting concepts in a similarly condensed format. This book focuses on understanding accounting as a reader of financial statements or as a business manager. *Mastering Financial Accounting Essentials* is a great book to use to round out your understanding of business financial results.

Stuart A. McCrary
August 2009

Acknowledgments

I would like to thank the many people at Chicago Partners LLC (a division of Navigant Consulting, Inc.) for their advice on presenting this corporate finance curriculum simply. In addition, I thank Paula Mikrut for making a careful reading of the text.

I also want to thank my students and the administration of Northwestern University, especially program directors Walter B. Herbst and Richard M. Lueptow. This book reflects my efforts to create an executive masters curriculum that covers topics in corporate finance in an incredibly short period. The class reflects our mutual efforts to present advanced financial information to nonfinance professionals so that these students can become more effective business leaders.

CHAPTER 1

Time Value of Money Toolbox

INTRODUCTION

One of the most important tools used in corporate finance is present value mathematics. These techniques are used to evaluate projects, make financial decisions, and evaluate investments. This chapter explains the time value of money, including present value (PV) and future value (FV), and how to adjust valuation formulas for various interest rate conventions. The chapter also presents several shortcuts to value a series of cash flows that fit a few standard patterns.

Readers should begin by developing an intuitive understanding of why it is necessary to incorporate interest rates into any analysis involving different periods of time. This understanding leads to a simple set of formulas expressing several time value relationships. After developing an intuitive understanding, readers will find it easy to incorporate interest rates by using the formulas for present value and/or future value in their analyses. Although this analysis shows up quite often, students will be relieved to find that its application is similar in most instances.

CASH FLOWS

Much of this text focuses on cash flows. Accountants realize the importance of cash; they devote an entire statement to the analysis of the sources and the uses of cash and cash balances. Accountants are interested in tracking cash flow in large measure because a company must have adequate cash to survive and prosper. Start-up companies may run out of cash before they have a chance to establish their businesses. Even established companies focus on both the profitability of the business and the flow of cash.

Corporate finance uses the same or similar measure of cash flow as accountants track in the statement of cash flows. However, this chapter and much of this book rely on cash flows for a completely different analysis and treat the cash flows from a project or even the cash flows of an entire corporation much like the cash flows of a bond. With a bond, investors transfer money today to borrowers, who in turn pay interest and eventually repay the loan. The size and timing of the cash payments and cash receipts determines the attractiveness of the bond investment. The techniques described herein will enable investors to evaluate the cash flows of any investment regardless of when the cash flows occur.

FUTURE VALUE

The future value of a cash flow is the value at some specified future time of a cash flow that occurs immediately. The concept of future value allows a company to decide whether cash flows that occur at two different times are equivalent. The way in which the two cash flows are equivalent is the subject of this chapter and will be explained subsequently.

Suppose that a company issues a bill that requires a customer to pay $100 upon receipt. The customer asks for extra time to pay. The company can borrow at an 8 percent interest rate. The company tells the customer that it will accept $102 instead in three months.

The company calculated the amount of cash it would accept that would be equivalent to getting $100 immediately. If the delay in receiving payment causes the company to borrow $100 for three months, the company must account for the interest on the loan. The formula for interest might look like Equation 1.1.

$$\text{Interest} = \$100 * 8\% * 3/12 = \$2 \qquad (1.1)$$

This is a formula for simple interest. Simple interest applies the interest rate to a principal balance for a period of time. The formula begins with the principal balance multiplied by the annual interest rate of 8 percent or $8. However, the rate applies only to three months or one-quarter of the year. Therefore, the interest for three months is $2, and the amount of the delayed payment would have to be $100 + 2 = $102 to compensate the company for the delay in payment.

The immediate payment of $100 in the preceding example is called the present value. The later payment is called a future value. As has been demonstrated, the two amounts are linked by the interest rate and the amount of time between the two payment dates.

In the preceding example, an 8 percent interest rate was used to determine an equivalent future payment from a present value. The method relied on a bank rate of interest. In fact, the company may still prefer the immediate payment of $100 to a deferred payment of $102. The deferred payment exposes the company to the risk of nonpayment for a longer period of time. The delay increases the amount the company must record as an account receivable in its financial statements and requires the company to include a liability on the balance sheet for the bank loan.

To address these concerns, the company may increase the interest rate used in determining the future value it will accept in lieu of the immediate payment of $100. Later, this text will explore factors that affect the interest rate or return that links present values to future values. This chapter, however, generally assumes that the company knows the required rate that incorporates these factors.

A more general formula for interest appears in Equation 1.2.

$$\text{Interest} = \text{Present Value} * \text{Rate} * \text{Time} \tag{1.2}$$

where Time is the interval in years between the time of the present value and the time of the future value and Rate is the annual interest rate.

The value of a cash payment that occurs immediately is the present value. The future value of this cash flow is the present value plus interest, as set forth in Equation 1.3.

$$\text{Future Value} = \text{Present Value} + \text{Interest} \tag{1.3}$$

Substitute the formula for interest in Equation 1.2 into the formula for future value in Equation 1.3 to produce Equation 1.4.

$$\text{Future Value} = \text{Present Value} + \text{Present Value} * \text{Rate} * \text{Time} \tag{1.4}$$

Finally, simplify Equation 1.4 by collecting terms. The result is Equation 1.5, which shows that the future value is related to the present value by a rate of interest that applies to the time from the present payments to the future payments.

$$\text{Future Value} = \text{Present Value} (1 + \text{Rate} * \text{Time}) \tag{1.5}$$

Compound Interest

The formula for future value in Equation 1.5 is correct for short intervals of time, but most investments pay interest every three months, every six months, or annually. When investments pay interest between the time of the present value and the time of the future value, the formula in Equation 1.5

is not correct. This section explains how these interim interest payments affect the calculation of the future value. First, it is necessary to explain the compounding process.

An old-fashioned passbook bank account illustrates the basic concepts of future value and compound interest. In the days before businesses had easy access to computers, banks used and reused a passbook as a simple ledger to account for customer deposits, withdrawals, and interest. Each time the customer deposited or withdrew funds, the new information was added to a running ledger. Modern monthly and quarterly statements work the same way, except that they include only a one-month or 3-month period of time. In contrast, the passbook included a running total of all deposits, withdrawals, and interest payments since the account was opened.

A customer could deposit an amount and see interest accumulate. Table 1.1 illustrates the process.

The investment of $1,000 on 3/14/20X1 grows to $1,040.28 by December 31, 20X1. In the absence of taxes, the cash amount on 3/14/20X1 is linked to the year-end balance of $1,040.28 by the amount of interest earned during the period.

The specific calculations in Table 1.1 require some explanation. In this example, interest is paid at the end of every calendar quarter. This example employs one commonly used method to calculate the number of days of interest—each month is assumed to have exactly 30 days and each year has 360 days. (See the appendix for a description of this method and other day-counting methods.) The first interest payment accumulates at 5 percent interest. If the rate applied for a full year (that is, the interest rate applied for a full year and was not compounded), the interest would be $50 ($1,000 times 5 percent). The interest for the 16-day period from March 14 to March 31 is a fraction of that annual amount equal to $50 ∗ 16/360 or $2.22.

The period from March 31 to June 30 contains exactly 91 actual days but the counting convention used here assumes there are 30 days in each month or 90 in each quarter. The interest for this quarter is $1,002.22 ∗ 5

TABLE 1.1   Passbook Investment at 5 Percent Quarterly Interest

Date	Deposit	Withdrawal	Days	Interest	Principal
03/14/20X1	1,000.00	—	—	—	1,000.00
03/31/20X1	—	—	16	2.22	1,002.22
06/30/20X1	—	—	90	12.53	1,014.75
09/30/20X1	—	—	90	12.68	1,027.43
12/31/20X1	—	—	90	12.84	1,040.28

percent $*$ 90/360 or $12.53. Notice that this old-fashioned way to count days calls for an interest payment of $12.53, whereas a more precise method would calculate $1,002.22 $*$ 91/365 or $12.49. The two values are generally fairly close, especially over a year or more. In some cases, the way interest is applied can have a big impact on the future value. It is important to understand the day-counting convention that is being used and to use the interest rate correctly.

Suppose a business orders some goods and could either pay the supplier $1,000 on March 14 or pay $1,040.28 at the end of the year when the goods will be delivered. Because the company can invest the $1,000 deposit, the customer could pay $1,000 now or invest the funds at 5 percent and pay $1,040.28 at year-end. Because the bank account provides exactly enough interest to pay the higher amount at the end of the year, the company does not prefer one alternative to the other. (Eventually, the comparison must include taxes and the risk of loss on the investment.)

Alternatively, the company could borrow $1,000 on March 14 at 5 percent and pay the lower invoice amount. The interest would accumulate to $1,040.28 by year-end. The company would need to pay $1,040.28 to repay the loan, which exactly equals the amount of the delayed payment.

A company cannot both borrow at 5 percent and invest at 5 percent as implied by the foregoing description. It is not necessary to be able to borrow and lend at the same rate. Rather, it is important to determine the relevant interest rate that can link the value on March 14 and the value on December 31. The calculation of future value using the appropriate interest rate provides a way to compare two different cash flows at different points in time.

The passbook investment detailed in Table 1.1 includes compound interest. In other words, the interest paid on March 31 also earns interest following that payment date. The value of the account rises on each payment date, and the base used to determine the interest payment is larger in later quarters. As a result, the interest payments are larger than if the bank had paid simple interest.

In contrast, if the bank paid simple interest on $1,000 using Equation 1.5, the customer would not benefit from earning interest on the quarterly interest payments. The interest rate would apply for 286/360 years or .794 years, taking the fraction of the year using the 30/360 day counting method shown in Table 1.1. The future value using Equation 1.5 would be

$$\text{Future Value} = \$1,000\,(1 + 5\% * .794) = \$1,039.72 \qquad (1.6)$$

Paying the customer quarterly (or even more frequent) interest has the effect of raising the return to the investor. It is important to follow the correct compounding assumption to determine the present or future value from a particular interest rate. This chapter will later address how to handle the difference in interest created by different compounding assumptions.

The formula for compound interest begins much like the formula for simple interest given in Equation 1.5. Suppose that the interest rate is 6 percent per year and an investment pays interest annually. The future value at the end of one year is shown in Equation 1.7.

$$FV_1 = PV * (1 + Rate * 1) = PV * (1 + Rate) \qquad (1.7)$$

After one year, a passbook would contain PV $*$ (1 + Rate). This amount from Equation 1.7 appears in Equation 1.8 in square brackets and is reinvested for another year.

$$FV_2 = [PV * (1 + Rate)] * (1 + Rate)$$
$$FV_2 = PV * (1 + Rate)^2 \qquad (1.8)$$

After two years, a passbook would contain PV $*$ (1 + Rate)^2. The amount from Equation 1.8 appears in Equation 1.9 in square brackets and is reinvested for another year.

$$FV_3 = \left[PV * (1 + Rate)^2 \right] * (1 + Rate)$$
$$FV_3 = PV * (1 + Rate)^3 \qquad (1.9)$$

Table 1.2 summarizes the growth in principal, now applying the specified rate of 6 percent and also showing the calculation of the interest generated in each period. In each case, the starting principal amount appears in the square brackets, and interest equals this updated principal amount times the annual interest rate.

The general formula for future value for an investment that pays annual interest appears in Equation 1.10.

$$FV_i = PV * (1 + Rate)^i \qquad (1.10)$$

where i equals the number of years between the present and the future.

TABLE 1.2 Passbook Investment at 6 Percent Annual Interest

Date	Principal	Interest	Interest
3/15/20X1	1,000,000	60,000	[Deposit] * (Rate)
3/15/20X2	1,060,000	63,600	[Deposit(1 + Rate)] * (Rate)
3/15/20X3	1,123,600	67,416	[Deposit(1 + Rate)(1 + Rate)] * (Rate)
3/15/20X4	1,191,016	71,461	[Deposit(1 + Rate)(1 + Rate)(1 + Rate)] * (Rate)

TABLE 1.3 Passbook Investment at 6 Percent Annual Interest

Date	Principal	Interest	
3/15/20X1	1,000,000	60,000	
3/15/20X2	1,060,000	63,600	
3/15/20X3	1,123,600	67,416	
3/15/20X4	1,191,016	35,730	(prorated 50 percent of annual interest)
9/15/20X4	1,226,746		

Equation 1.10 makes it easy to calculate the future value for much longer periods without needing to calculate individual interest payments as was done in Table 1.2.

Some care should be exercised in using Equation 1.10 for fractional periods. For example, the future value after 3.5 years could be calculated successively, as in Table 1.3. In this case, the interest is prorated for half of a year.

Applying Equation 1.10 for the fractional period of 3.5 years yields approximately the same answer:

$$FV_{3.5} = PV * (1 + .06)^{3.5} = 1,226,226 \quad\quad (1.11)$$

More Frequent Compounding

Equations 1.7 to 1.10 develop a general formula for compounding an investment that pays interest annually. Most U.S. bonds, along with many other instruments, pay interest twice each year. Equation 1.12 shows the future value of a cash flow one year in the future for investments that pay interest twice each year:

$$
\begin{aligned}
\text{Future Value}_1 &= \text{Present Value} * \left(1 + \frac{\text{Rate}}{2}\right) * \left(1 + \frac{\text{Rate}}{2}\right) \\
&= \text{Present Value} * \left(1 + \frac{\text{Rate}}{2}\right)^2
\end{aligned}
\quad\quad (1.12)
$$

The term in the first set of parentheses adjusts the starting present value to the middle of the year using simple interest, much like the adjustment in Equation 1.5. Then the original amount plus the interest collected in six months is reinvested. The term in the second set of parentheses adjusts the starting present value plus interest from the first semiannual interest payment to the end of the year.

The future value one year in the future of a cash flow for investments that pay interest quarterly is presented in Equation 1.13.

$$FV_1 = PV * \left(1 + \frac{Rate}{4}\right) * \left(1 + \frac{Rate}{4}\right) * \left(1 + \frac{Rate}{4}\right) * \left(1 + \frac{Rate}{4}\right)$$

$$= PV * \left(1 + \frac{Rate}{4}\right)^4 \tag{1.13}$$

Like Equation 1.12 for semiannual interest, the year is divided into subperiods. At the end of each subperiod, the investment pays interest and the interest is available to be reinvested. Equation 1.14 presents a more general formula that can account for rates that compound at difference frequencies.

$$FV_{Years} = PV * \left(1 + \frac{Rate}{Freq}\right)^{Years*Freq} \tag{1.14}$$

where Years represents the time between the present and the future value date and Freq refers to the number of compounding periods per year.

For example, an annual bond has a frequency or Freq of one. In this case, Equation 1.14 simplifies to Equation 1.10. A semiannual bond would use 2 for Freq, and there would be twice as many semiannual periods and years between the present and the future value date. Two other common frequencies are quarterly for many money market instruments and monthly for mortgage investments. Banks may pay interest with daily compounding, in which case Freq would be 365 or 366. Finally, the shortest possible compounding period could be a tiny fraction of a year. Compounding over infinitesimally small compounding periods, called continuous compounding, is discussed further along in the text.

THE IMPACT OF COMPOUNDING FREQUENCY ON FUTURE VALUE

Interest on interest increases the effective interest rate. In other words, compound interest raises the future value compared to simple interest. In general, the more frequently interest is compounded, the higher the effective interest rate and the higher the resulting future value.

Table 1.4 begins with a present value of $1,000. The interest rate is 6 percent and the future value 10 years later is determined for simple

TABLE 1.4 Compounding Frequency at 6 Percent Interest

Frequency	Description	Future Value
0	Simple	1,600.00
1	Annual	1,790.85
2	Semiannual	1,806.11
4	Quarterly	1,814.02
12	Monthly	1,819.40
365	Daily	1,822.03
∞	Continuous	1,822.12

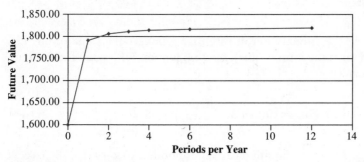

FIGURE 1.1 Future Value versus Compounding Frequency

interest (no compounding), and several commonly assumed compounding frequencies.

The data is presented visually in Figure 1.1, which plots the future value for simple interest and various compounding frequencies.

The important point to remember is that it is necessary to know what compounding assumptions are associated with the rate of interest used in present value and future value calculations and to develop a value using the correct assumption.

EQUIVALENT INTEREST RATE

More frequent compounding has the same effect as using a higher interest rate. That is, for a given present value, the future value increases as the assumed interest rate rises. The future value also increases as the compounding frequency rises.

Not surprisingly, market participants adjust downward the stated rates of frequently compounded interest rates to compensate for the larger amount of interest on interest earned with frequent compounding. It is often necessary to determine how much to adjust a particular rate to produce the same results as a different interest rate with a different compounding frequency.

Suppose a 10 percent quarterly-compounded interest rate is used—that is, the interest rate for one year is 10 percent so that interest of 2.5 percent is paid quarterly. By applying Equation 1.14, it is possible to determine the annually compounded rate that is equivalent.

Applying Equation 1.14 to a $100 present value for one year, the future value would be $110.38 as shown in Equation 1.15.

$$FV_4 = 100 * \left(1 + \frac{10\%}{4}\right)^4 = 110.38 \tag{1.15}$$

To determine the annual interest rate that produces the same result (i.e., produces in the same future value), set up Equation 1.14 again for an annually compounded rate.

$$FV_1 = 100 * \left(1 + \frac{Rate_1}{1}\right)^1 = 110.38 \tag{1.16}$$

It is easy to see that the annually-compounded rate of 10.38 percent would produce the same future value as a 10 percent rate compounded quarterly. The rate calculated from Equation 1.16 is called the equivalent annual rate or the effective annual rate. (Note that the "annual percentage rate" that mortgage lenders are required to disclose to borrowers is not the same. That rate includes the impact of certain loan origination costs not included here.)

To calculate an equivalent semiannual rate, set up Equation 1.14 again for two compounding periods per year.

$$FV_2 = 100 * \left(1 + \frac{Rate_2}{2}\right)^2 = 110.38 \tag{1.17}$$

This rate is a bit more challenging to calculate. By manipulating a few terms in Equation 1.17, it is possible to solve for the equivalent semiannual rate.

$$\left(1 + \frac{Rate_2}{2}\right)^2 = \frac{110.38}{100} \tag{1.18}$$

Simplify the right side with division and take the square root of both sides as shown in Equation 1.19.

$$\left(1 + \frac{\text{Rate}_2}{2}\right) = \sqrt{1.1038} \tag{1.19}$$

Finally, rearrange with a little more algebra.

$$\text{Rate}_2 = 2\left(\sqrt{1.1038} - 1\right) = 10.125\% \tag{1.20}$$

The equations in this book evaluated with more decimal points of accuracy than appear on the page. Equation 1.20 equals 10.124 percent using the values printed due to rounding.

This method converts a rate with one compounding frequency to an equivalent rate with a different compounding frequency by determining the rate that produces the same future value as the future value associated with the known beginning rate.

CONTINUOUSLY COMPOUNDED INTEREST

Figure 1.1 makes clear that more frequent compounding results in a higher future value (or equivalently, a higher effective interest rate). Figure 1.1 also suggests that the impact of more frequent compounding has a larger impact going from one to two to four compounding periods than the impact of compounding more frequently than monthly. Table 1.4 demonstrates that, for a given annual rate, daily compounding produces a higher future value than monthly compounding, but the impact is smaller. Compounding more frequently than daily produces very little difference in the future value or the effective interest rate.

Although the impact is small, many people use interest rates that are continuously compounded. Continuously compounded rates assume that interest is paid and reinvested after each infinitesimally small step in time. These rates are used not to raise the effective interest rate but instead to simplify the math. For example, option pricing formulas that use continuously compounded rates may be simpler or easier to apply than rates with other compounding frequencies.

The future value of a cash flow using continuous compounding is shown in Equation 1.21.

$$\text{FV}_{\text{Continuous}} = \text{PV} * e^{\text{Rate}*\text{Time}} \tag{1.21}$$

TABLE 1.5   Future Value at 6 Percent Continuous Compounding

Time	Future Value	Excel Syntax
0	100.00	=100*exp(6%*0)
1	106.18	=100*exp(6%*1)
2	112.75	=100*exp(6%*2)
5	134.99	=100*exp(6%*5)
10	182.21	=100*exp(6%*10)

where Rate is a continuously compounded interest rate, Time again measures the difference in years between the future valuing date and the present, and e refers to the mathematical constant equal to 2.718.

Questions and answers that follow at the end of the chapter will use the continuously compounded rate and provide a more complete explanation of how to use continuous compounding. For a short explanation, refer to Table 1.5, which lists the future value of $100 for several years at 6 percent interest along with the syntax for instructing Excel to produce these values.

It is clear from the line in Table 1.5 showing the future value after one year that a 6 percent continuously compounded rate is equivalent to a 6.18 percent annually compounded rate.

PRESENT VALUE

So far, this chapter has introduced ways to find a value in the future that is worth the same as a cash payment that occurs immediately. Consider, now, the case of a single payment you must make one month (30 days) in the future. Assume the payment equals $1 million.* Suppose as well that you could make a somewhat smaller payment immediately instead of paying $1 million 30 days from now. The annual interest rate is 10 percent.

You may pay either $1 million in a month or $991,735.54 today. The interest in this case was calculated by multiplying a smaller amount (PV) times an interest rate of 10 percent. If the payment were deferred for an entire year, the interest would equal PV * 10 percent. In the preceding case, the annual interest rate was reduced to a daily rate by dividing by 360, the days per year in the 30/360 counting convention. Finally, the daily amount

---

*Later, it will be convenient to present the values in terms of a nominal $1.00 cash flow. The advantage of working with $1 in each case is that all results can then be simply multiplied by the relevant actual cash flows.

was converted to monthly by multiplying by 30. The calculation of interest is described in Equation 1.22.

$$\text{Interest} = \frac{\text{PV} * 10\% * 30}{360} \tag{1.22}$$

In the preceding example and in general, the 10 percent annual interest rate was reduced by the fraction of the year involved in the calculation. Equation 1.22 could be modified to reflect a different day counting convention. The appendix presents a brief description of day-counting alternatives.

The payment of PV plus the interest in 30 days must equal $1,000,000. Equation 1.23 shows how to calculate the immediate payment that is equivalent to $1,000,000 a month from now.

$$\$1,000,000 = \text{PV} + \frac{\text{PV} * 10\% * 30}{360}$$

$$\$1,000,000 = \text{PV} * \left(1 + \frac{10\% * 30}{360}\right)$$

$$\text{PV} = \frac{\$1,000,000}{1 + \dfrac{10\% * 30}{360}} = \$991,735.54 \tag{1.23}$$

If you have the money to pay the invoice now, you could pay the immediate amount of $991,735.54 or make the payment of $1,000,000 in 30 days. If you postpone payment and invest the money in a short-term investment (also at 10 percent), you will earn exactly enough to pay the later, higher amount.* If you really can earn exactly 10 percent, you should be completely indifferent as to whether you pay $991,735.54 now or $1,000,000 in a month from now.†

Alternatively, the company may prefer to borrow money now to make the immediate payment. If the cost of borrowing were 10 percent, you would owe $8,264.46 in interest ($991,735.54 * 10 percent * 30/360) if

---

*Again, taxes complicate the matter, of course. See Equations 1.28 and 1.29.
†Accountants would record the alternatives differently. They would recognize the explicit interest as interest revenue. They would not impute an interest expense for the deferred payment. Instead, they would likely record a higher cost of goods sold. Nevertheless, as long as the delayed payment amount is based on (exactly) the same interest rate as the earning rate, net income would be equal regardless of whether the company paid early or later.

you make an early payment while avoiding an equal charge on the invoice amount. The company must repay principal of $991,735.54 plus interest of $8,264.46 after 30 days, a total of $1 million. As long as the implicit interest rate on the invoice matches your borrowing rate, it doesn't matter whether you make an early payment or a payment in 30 days.

By similar logic, your creditor is indifferent between receiving $991,735.54 immediately or $1 million in a month. If your creditor is a net borrower, it will incur additional borrowing costs of $8,264.46, because your delay in payment results in a larger loan balance for the creditor for a month (if the creditor borrows at 10 percent). Alternatively, if your early payment means your creditor has $991,735.54 more invested in interest-bearing investments, those investments would earn $8,264.46 over 30 days. Although the creditor receives $8,264.46 less from the customer, the creditor receives $8,264.46 additional interest income.

The interest calculated this way is not correct for longer time intervals. Contractual payments can extend over several years. For these uses, a compound interest method that calculates interest over years or even decades is required.

In all the preceding examples, both you and your company were able to either borrow or invest at the same rate. That is, of course, not realistic. In fact, trade credit is often a major motivation for sales. Large creditworthy manufacturers can pass some of their borrowing advantage on to customers as a sales inducement.

For the purposes of describing the time value of money, however, it is convenient to start with the simplifying assumption that everyone agrees on the interest rate. In the preceding examples, both you and your creditor are indifferent between an early payment and a larger payment 30 days later. If we calculate the future amount from an immediate cash flow, it is called a future value. The amount we could accept as immediate payment in lieu of a payment sometime in the future is called the present value. (See Figures 1.2 and 1.3.)

The present values of future cash flows are often called discounted cash flows because the present value is less than the actual cash flows occurring in the future. When an investment is valued from forecasted future cash flows and the future cash flows are all converted to present values, the analysis is called discounted cash flow analysis.

FORMULAS FOR PRESENT VALUE AND FUTURE VALUE

The general formula for the future value of an immediate cash flow appears in Equation 1.24.

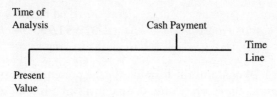

FIGURE 1.2 Present Value Time Line

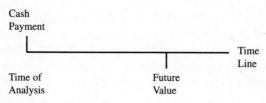

FIGURE 1.3 Future Value Time Line

$$FV = \text{Cash Flow} \, (1 + \text{Rate})^{\text{Time}} \quad \text{(Equation 1.10 restated slightly)} \quad (1.24)$$

where Rate is the annual interest rate used and Time is the number of years until the future date. To repeat, this formula applies to interest rates that pay interest annually.

The general formula for the present value of a future payment appears in Equation 1.25.

$$PV = \frac{\text{Cash Flow}}{(1 + \text{Rate})^{\text{Time}}} \quad (1.25)$$

where Rate is the annual interest rate used and Time is the number of years until the future date. Equation 1.25 is derived from Equation 1.24 by rearranging the times to adjust the value of a future cash flow back to the present instead of adjusting the value of an immediate cash flow to the future.

As with Equation 1.24, this formula applies to interest rates that pay interest annually. The formula can be altered in the same way that Equation 1.14 was modified to apply rates of different compounding periods by modifying the way the formula handles the rate and the number of compounding periods.

■ **Example 1:** What is the present value of a payment of $40,000 made in 2.5 years if the annual interest rate is 8 percent?

$$PV = \frac{\$40,000}{(1 + .08)^{2.5}} = 32,998.99 \qquad (1.26)$$

Equation 1.26 contains the formula for the present value of Example 1. If 8 percent is the interest rate, the payment of $40,000 in 2.5 years is worth only as much as an immediate payment of $32,998.99.
■ **Example 2:** What is the future value of a payment of $25,000 made in four years if the annual interest rate is 6 percent?

$$FV = 25,000 * (1 + .06)^4 = 31,561.92 \qquad (1.27)$$

Equation 1.27 contains the formula for the future value of Example 2. Faced with a 4-year delay in receiving payment, you should insist on receiving $31,561.92 instead of an immediate payment of $25,000.

Taxes can easily be incorporated into the present value and future value models. Suppose that a corporation pays a marginal tax rate of 35 percent. This effectively lowers the corporation's borrowing cost by 35 percent, since an interest expense lowers taxable income and tax payments should go down by 35 percent of the interest expense. Similarly, the net return on an investment is 35 percent lower than the indicated interest rate.

To apply after-tax analysis to discounted cash flows, you could reduce the effective interest rate. For example, if interest rates are 10 percent and a corporation pays a 35 percent corporate income tax rate, the after-tax interest rate is 10 percent * (100 percent − 35 percent) = 6.5 percent.

The impact of corporate taxes effectively lowers the interest rate. The formulas for present value and future value can account for the impact of taxes on value. See Equations 1.28 and 1.29.

$$PV = \frac{1}{[1 + (1 - \text{Tax}) * \text{Rate}]^{\text{Time}}} \qquad (1.28)$$

$$FV = [1 + (1 - \text{Tax}) * \text{Rate}]^{\text{Time}} \qquad (1.29)$$

In the preceding formulas, a $1 nominal cash flow was assumed in each case. The marginal corporate tax rate is included as "Tax." These formulations also assume that the cash flow is not a taxable cash flow or that the values from the formulas will be applied to cash flows already reduced by taxes.

The present value and future value models are tools that can be used to make certain financial decisions within a firm. One direct application is to compare alternative payment options as described previously. The company should select the alternative that maximizes shareholder value. The company should select the alternative that is cheaper when the appropriate discount rate is used.*

The present value and future value models can also assess simple investment alternatives. The formulas provide a basis for comparing a variety of simple investments (a single outflow at the beginning and a single, certain return later). These techniques are used frequently to evaluate a series of investments in order to ration scarce capital and invest in the most attractive alternatives.

CONCLUSION

The first step in reviewing cash flows is to make all individual cash flows equivalent. The largest impact is usually the adjustment for the time value of money. Present value and future value formulas provide a basis for comparing and combining the value of cash flows occurring at different times.

---

* Choosing the appropriate discount rate (also called the firm's cost of capital) is not a trivial matter. Many factors enter the calculation of the cost of capital, including the riskiness of the firm, the riskiness of a particular project, whether a new investment reduces or increases existing business risks, market risks, and more. Chapter 3 presents financial theories useful in determining the appropriate discount rate.

1.1. Your supplier asks you to pay your $300,000 invoice in 30 days. However, the supplier will allow you to pay $298,500 immediately. You can borrow at 5 percent (annual rate). Should you pay $298,500 immediately or $300,000 in 30 days? Ignore any impact of taxes.

1.2. Ignoring any impact of taxes, what borrowing rate would make you indifferent between paying the invoice in Question 1.1 immediately and paying $300,000 in a month?

1.3a. If you deposit money today into an account that pays 6.5 percent interest, how long will it take you to double your money if interest does not compound (simple annual interest)?

1.3b. If interest compounds annually?

1.3c. If interest compounds semiannually?

1.3d. If interest compounds quarterly?

1.3e. If interest compounds continuously?

1.4a. What is the daily compounded rate equivalent to a semiannual 6 percent rate?

1.4b. What is the monthly compounded rate equivalent to a 6 percent semiannual rate?

1.4c. What is the annually compounded rate equivalent to a semiannual 6 percent rate?

1.4d. What is the continuously compounded rate equivalent to a semiannual 6 percent rate?

1.5. Following a large decline in stock prices, David commented that he lost 100 percent of the value of his 401K; then he grinned and added, "continuously compounded." If David's 401K was worth $100,000 18 months ago, what is it worth today?

CHAPTER 2

Statistics for Finance

INTRODUCTION

This chapter describes some of the statistics used in finance. The topics covered are only a part of the whole range of statistics, and the discussion is not intended to be comprehensive. Instead, it provides a summary of measures of variability or uncertainty.

To understand most of the ideas that are contained in the following chapters, the reader must have a strong background in statistics. This knowledge will be helpful in studying investment risk as used by portfolio managers and in making investment decisions.

Much of the finance literature assumes that investment returns are normally distributed—that is, that the returns can be described by the familiar "bell curve." To use the normal distribution, the user must set two parameters so that the most likely outcomes in the normal distribution are consistent with actual or predicted returns and can be used to determine the likelihood of returns higher and lower than expected. To make sense of the normal distribution, it is helpful to start with a description of the mean and standard deviation.

THE MEANING OF MEAN OR AVERAGE

Add up all the observations and divide by the number of observations. In most applications, each observation is equally weighted. The formula in Equation 2.1 is simply:*

---

* Other terms used for the center of the distribution are the *median* and the *mode*. Half of the observations are larger and half are smaller than the median. The mode is the value most frequently found in the data series.

$$\bar{r} = \frac{\sum r}{N} \tag{2.1}$$

where r is any random variable (such as return) and N is a count of the number of r values observed.

When all possible outcomes for the variable are included in the average, the statistic is called the population mean. When a portion of all possible values is averaged (also called a sample), the mean is called a sample mean.

When the values are weighted, the mean is as shown in Equation 2.2.

$$\bar{r} = \sum_{i=1}^{N} w_i * r_i \tag{2.2}$$

where $\Sigma w_i = 1$ or 100 percent.

For example, if 60 percent of the merchandise in inventory is in 32-ounce containers and 40 percent of the merchandise in inventory is in 64-ounce containers, the average or mean of the volume is $60\% * 32 + 40\% * 64$ or 44.8 ounces.

In the case of the weighted mean, it may or may not be possible to count all the observations. Equation 2.2 can calculate the mean when the frequency at which each value occurs is known.

It is convenient to think of the mean as a method to summarize the data being studied. The mean describes the general magnitude of the observations. Because an individual observation may not be typical, the mean might be a more reliable measure of the general magnitude of the observations than individual observations.

MEDIAN AS A SUBSTITUTE FOR MEAN

The median is an alternative to the mean for establishing the general magnitude of data. The median is the point in a population or sample for which half of the remaining data is larger than the median and half of the remaining data is smaller than the median. In many cases, the mean and the median are approximately equal.

Most applications of statistics in finance use the mean rather than the median. The examples in this book use the mean in all cases.

STANDARD DEVIATION MEASURES THE NOISE

The mean simplifies a collection of observations, but much of the detail is lost. Without seeing the individual observations, it is impossible to tell

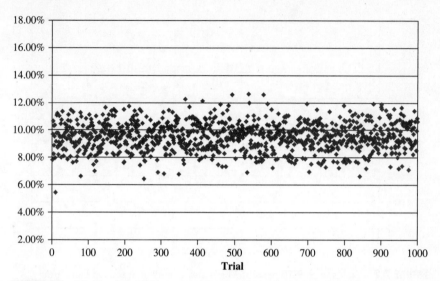

FIGURE 2.1 Yields with 9.50 percent Mean and 1 percent Standard Deviation

whether most observations are approximately equal to the mean or whether they vary tremendously. The most common measures of dispersion are *variance* and the closely related statistic called *standard deviation*. The observations in Figure 2.1 spread out over a mean of 9.5 percent. In fact, observations near 9.5 percent (including values slightly above and slightly below 9.5 percent) are the most commonly occurring observations. Observations below 8.5 percent or above 10.5 percent occur less frequently. Observations below 7.5 percent or above 11.5 percent are rare.

Figure 2.2 shows a similar set of observations. These observations are also centered around a mean of 9.5 percent. However, observations 1 or 2 percent above or below the mean are common.

Table 2.1 is a histogram of the 1,000 returns used to create Figure 2.1 and Figure 2.2. The first line contains a return of 2.5 percent followed by a count of zero instances of a return of 2.5 percent or lower in both Figures 2.1 and 2.2. The following line contains a count of the number of returns between 2.5 percent and 3.5 percent. Figure 2.1 contains no returns between 2.5 percent and 3.5 percent, but Figure 2.2 contains four returns in that range.

Notice that the number of returns close to 9.5 percent is higher for the returns in Figure 2.1 than for those in Figure 2.2.

Figure 2.3 displays the count of returns in Table 2.1 visually. As with Table 2.1, it is clear that the returns in Figure 2.2 span a wider range. In other words, although the returns average about 9.5 percent in both cases,

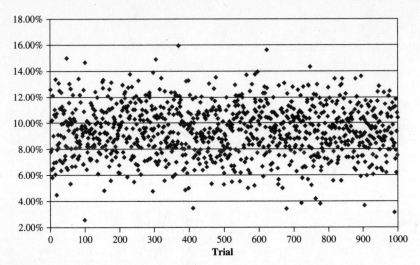

FIGURE 2.2   Yields with 9.50 percent Mean and 2 percent Standard Deviation

the chance that a return differs from the mean is much higher for the data in Figure 2.2 than for the data in Figure 2.1.

There are several measures of the extent of this dispersion. Imagine summing up all the vertical distances between an individual observation and the 9.5 percent mean. You would have to add the positive differences

TABLE 2.1   Count of Returns by Range

Return	Figure 2.1	Figure 2.2
2.50%	0	0
3.50%	0	4
4.50%	0	5
5.50%	1	14
6.50%	1	43
7.50%	22	108
8.50%	127	145
9.50%	320	193
10.50%	358	187
11.50%	147	151
12.50%	21	96
13.50%	3	41
14.50%	0	8
15.50%	0	3
16.50%	0	2

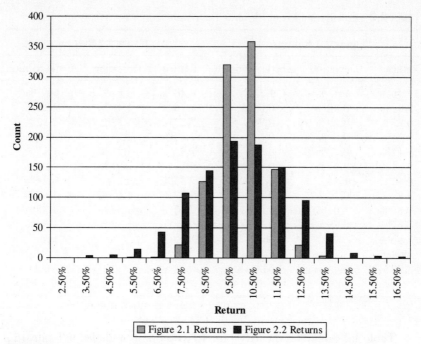

FIGURE 2.3   Histogram of Returns

between each observation and the mean (i.e., the absolute value of each distance), because otherwise the differences would cancel out. The mean absolute deviation averages this vertical distance from the mean. The standard deviation first squares each value (i.e., each observation is multiplied times itself). Figures 2.1 and 2.2 include an indication of these two measures of this dispersion.

The mean absolute deviation (MAD) calculates each of these deviations from the mean and averages the positive differences from the mean. The statistic is defined in Equation 2.3.

$$\text{MAD} = \frac{\sum\limits_{i=1}^{N} |r_i - \bar{r}|}{N} \tag{2.3}$$

Equation 2.3 starts with the differences between individual observations and the mean (or alternatively between the observations and the median). The MAD is the mean of the absolute value of these differences (i.e., the value ignoring the negative or minus sign).

TABLE 2.2   Calculating Mean Absolute Deviation

Figure 2.1 Returns			Figure 2.2 Returns		
Return	Deviation	Abs(Deviation)	Return	Deviation	Abs(Deviation)
11.40%	1.52%	1.52%	8.43%	−0.67%	0.67%
9.08%	−0.80%	0.80%	11.26%	2.16%	2.16%
10.67%	0.79%	0.79%	7.27%	−1.82%	1.82%
9.24%	−0.64%	0.64%	11.83%	2.74%	2.74%
9.11%	−0.77%	0.77%	7.92%	−1.17%	1.17%
9.21%	−0.67%	0.67%	6.18%	−2.91%	2.91%
8.52%	−1.35%	1.35%	9.34%	0.24%	0.24%
9.97%	0.10%	0.10%	10.77%	1.67%	1.67%
10.89%	1.02%	1.02%	7.52%	−1.58%	1.58%
10.67%	0.79%	0.79%	10.42%	1.33%	1.33%
Average		Sum	Average		Sum
9.88%		8.44%	9.09%		16.29%
		MAD			MAD
		0.94%			1.81%

Table 2.2 calculates the MAD for 10 data points included in Figures 2.1 and 2.2.

The first column lists 10 returns from Figure 2.1. These returns average 9.88 percent, the mean return in Equation 2.3. Notice that these 10 returns do not closely match the 9.5 percent return calculated from the 1,000 returns shown in Figure 2.1.

The second column of Table 2.2 lists the difference between each of the returns in the first column and the average return of 9.88 percent. Notice that the values may be greater or less than zero. The third column changes the negative deviations to positive (i.e., the third column is the absolute value of the deviations in the second column). These values in the third column sum to 8.44 percent. The MAD is 8.44 percent divided by $N-1$ (rather than N because this is a sample, not a population of all possibilities) or 0.94 percent.

The fourth column of Table 2.2 lists 10 returns from Figure 2.2. These returns average 9.09 percent—again not a very close match to the average of all 1,000 returns plotted in Figure 2.2. This average is used to calculate the deviations in the fifth column. Column six removes the negative signs. The sum of these absolute deviations is 16.29 percent. The MAD equals 16.29 percent divided by 9, or 1.81 percent.

The MAD provides a precise way to measure the amount of variability around the mean. For the 10 data points used in the example in Table 2.2, the MAD calculated from the returns in Figure 2.2 is about twice as large as the MAD calculated from the returns in Figure 2.1.

Two related measures, variance and standard deviation, are more commonly used measures of the differences between the mean and individual values. Variance is the average of these squared distances. Standard deviation rescales those results back to about the size of the original deviations (see Figures 2.1 and 2.2).

Equation 2.4a is the formula for the variance of a population, and Equation 2.4b is the formula for sample variance.

$$\sigma^2 = \frac{\sum_{i=1}^{N} (r_i - \bar{r})^2}{N} \tag{2.4a}$$

$$s^2 = \frac{\sum_{i=1}^{N} (r_i - \bar{r})^2}{N - 1} \tag{2.4b}$$

Variance is usually labeled σ^2 for the population variance and s^2 for the sample variance. Equation 2.4b divides the sum of the squared differences from the mean by one less than the number of data points in the calculation. Since Equation 2.4a describes the population variance, all data points are included, and the result of Equation 2.4a is an exact answer. The result of Equation 2.4b, the sample variance, is an estimate of the population variance. Very commonly, only sample data is available, so Equation 2.4b is used to measure the sample variance (s^2) to estimate the population variance (σ^2). Most of the models that rely on variance in this book (or on the closely related statistic standard deviation described below) use the Greek letter sigma (σ) for the population statistic, but that value may be estimated with Equation 2.4b or Equation 2.5b.

Notice that standard deviation equals the square root of variance. The standard deviation is obtained using nearly the identical calculation as in Equations 2.4a and 2.4b. The formula for the standard deviation is displayed in Equations 2.5a and 2.5b.

$$\sigma = \sqrt{\frac{\sum_{i=1}^{N} (r_i - \bar{r})^2}{N}} \tag{2.5a}$$

The Greek letter sigma (σ) is usually used as a symbol for the standard deviation of a population. The formula in Equation 2.5a is the population standard deviation; it should be used when all possible values are available to calculate the standard deviation.

When a subset or sample of all possible values is used, Equation 2.5a is modified slightly. (See Equation 2.5b.) The standard deviation of a sample is usually represented with the letter s rather than σ.

$$s = \sqrt{\frac{\sum\limits_{i=1}^{N}(r_i - \bar{r})^2}{N-1}} \qquad (2.5b)$$

To calculate the variance using Equation 2.4b, the average return is subtracted from individual returns and then squared. These differences are also called squared deviations. The individual squared deviations are averaged (with the minor detail of the subtraction of 1 in the denominator). Variance is then rescaled back to the original magnitude by taking the square root and calling it standard deviation. Therefore, notwithstanding two adjustments (the squaring of the deviations and dividing by $N-1$ instead of N), the standard deviation is similar to the MAD and is closely related to the average of the distance (i.e., the positive difference) between a typical data point and the average.

The first column of Table 2.3 again lists 10 returns from Figure 2.1. These returns average 9.88 percent—the mean return in Equation 2.4b and the same average calculated in Table 2.2.

The second column of Table 2.3 again lists the difference between each of the returns in the first column and the average return of 9.88 percent. As with Table 2.2, this column contains both positive and negative values. The third column squares the deviations. As a result, all these squared deviations are also positive. These values in the third column sum to 0.085 percent. The variance is 0.085 percent divided by $N-1$, or 0.009 percent. The standard deviation is the square root of .009 percent, or 0.974 percent.

The fourth column of Table 2.3 repeats the 10 returns from Figure 2.2, also listed in Table 2.3. These returns again average 9.09 percent. This average is used to calculate the deviations in the fifth column. Column six squares the values in the fifth column. The sum of these squared deviations is 0.329 percent. The variance equals 0.329 percent divided by 9 or 0.037 percent. The standard deviation is the square root of 0.037 percent or 1.911 percent.

The variance and standard deviation provide two additional measures of the variability around the mean. For the 10 data points used in the example in Table 2.3, the standard deviation calculated from the returns in Figure 2.2 is about twice as large as the standard deviation calculated from the returns in Figure 2.1. The variance of the returns in Figure 2.2 is about four times larger than the variance of returns in Figure 2.1.

TABLE 2.3   Calculating Variance and Standard Deviation

	Figure 2.1			Figure 2.2	
Return	Deviation	Deviation²	Return	Deviation	Deviation²
11.40%	1.52%	0.023%	8.43%	−0.67%	0.004%
9.08%	−0.80%	0.006%	11.26%	2.16%	0.047%
10.67%	0.79%	0.006%	7.27%	−1.82%	0.033%
9.24%	−0.64%	0.004%	11.83%	2.74%	0.075%
9.11%	−0.77%	0.006%	7.92%	−1.17%	0.014%
9.21%	−0.67%	0.004%	6.18%	−2.91%	0.085%
8.52%	−1.35%	0.018%	9.34%	0.24%	0.001%
9.97%	0.10%	0.000%	10.77%	1.67%	0.028%
10.89%	1.02%	0.010%	7.52%	−1.58%	0.025%
10.67%	0.79%	0.006%	10.42%	1.33%	0.018%
Average		Sum	Average		Sum
9.88%		0.085%	9.09%		0.329%
		Variance			Variance
		0.009%			0.037%
		Standard			Standard
		Deviation			Deviation
		0.974%			1.911%

The data in Figure 2.1 include 1,000 samples and have a mean of 9.54 percent and a standard deviation of 1.02 percent. The Figure 2.1 sample corresponds closely with the population average of 9.5 percent and a standard deviation of 1 percent. The data in Figure 2.2 have a mean of 9.43 percent and a standard deviation of 1.97 percent. The Figure 2.2 sample corresponds closely with the population average of 9.5 percent and a standard deviation of 2 percent.

Although this standard deviation is twice as high as the standard deviation of the data in Figure 2.1, the data still center around 9.5 percent and are clustered near that mean, but not as tightly as the data in Figure 2.1. Taken together, the mean and the standard deviation summarize the magnitude of the observations and the general level of dispersion.

ANNUALIZING VARIANCE AND STANDARD DEVIATION ESTIMATES

The data series may be observed daily, monthly, or annually. A calculation of variance using annual data will be higher than the same calculation performed on monthly or daily data. For data such as securities prices or interest rates, it is typical for the variance calculated from annual returns to be approximately 12 times larger than the variance calculated from monthly returns.* Similarly, the monthly variance will be 20–22 times larger than the variance of daily returns (if there are 20–22 business days in a month).

Therefore:

$$\sigma^2_{\text{Annual}} = 12 * \sigma^2_{\text{Monthly}} = 251 * \sigma^2_{\text{Daily}} \qquad (2.6a)$$

Note that there are about 251 days per year when markets are open. The number of business days per year differs around the world, and practitioners may make slightly different assumptions in adjusting variance and standard deviations for the length of time.

Since the standard deviation is the square root of the variance in Equation 2.6a, Equation 2.6b shows the relationship between the standard deviation of data observed annually, monthly, and daily.

$$\sqrt{\sigma^2_{\text{Annual}}} = \sqrt{12 * \sigma^2_{\text{Monthly}}} = \sqrt{251 * \sigma^2_{\text{Daily}}} \qquad (2.6b)$$

When simplified, Equation 2.6c shows that the standard deviation measured annually can be estimated from data observed daily or monthly if the daily and monthly measurements are adjusted by the square root of the measure of time.

$$\sigma_{\text{Annual}} = \sqrt{12} * \sigma_{\text{Monthly}} = \sqrt{251} * \sigma_{\text{Daily}} \qquad (2.6c)$$

The Normal Distribution

The familiar "bell curve" (also known as the Gaussian distribution) is commonly used in finance. Most of us first heard about the normal distribution when a teacher explained why there had to be an uncomfortably large number of C's in a particular class and a surprisingly small number of A's. In short, most of the class was getting a B because our grades were clustered together. The normal curve recognizes that tendency for data to fall close together near the mean.

This distribution is used in science, industry, and the social sciences, because real data very often look a lot like the normal distribution. Mathematically, the formula is Equation 2.7.

$$f(x, \mu, \sigma) = \frac{1}{\sqrt{2x}\sigma} e^{-\left(\frac{(x-\mu)^2}{2\sigma^2}\right)} \qquad (2.7)$$

---

*Actual data tend to show a little higher variance for annual intervals compared to measures over shorter periods.

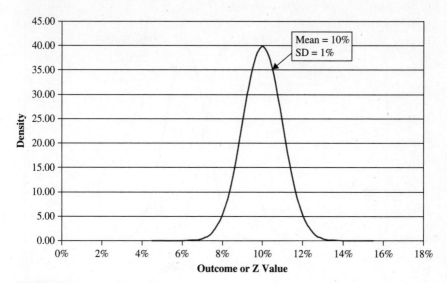

FIGURE 2.4A Normal Distribution

This formula means that the value of the function (represented by "f") depends on some data point (represented by "x"), the average or mean (represented by the Greek letter mu, "μ"), and the standard deviation (represented by the Greek letter sigma, "σ"). These are the same mean and standard deviation described previously.

For the normal distribution, the mean is the center of the distribution. For this reason, it is easy to see how the mean determines the location of the bell curve. Figure 2.4A depicts a normal curve centered on a mean of 10 percent. To move the bell curve right or left, change the mean. The two curves in Figure 2.4B reflect just a change in the general size (i.e., the means) of the two sets of data. The data represented by the curve on the left averages 8 percent whereas the data represented by the curve on the right averages 10 percent. Each set of data is similarly dispersed around the two means or averages.

THE NORMAL CURVE IS A PROBABILITY DISTRIBUTION

Mathematicians use many words that mean approximately the same thing. The normal curve is frequently called the bell curve outside the classroom. Mathematicians also call it the Gauss function (after the mathematician Carl Friedrich Gauss). It is also called the "density" function. The density

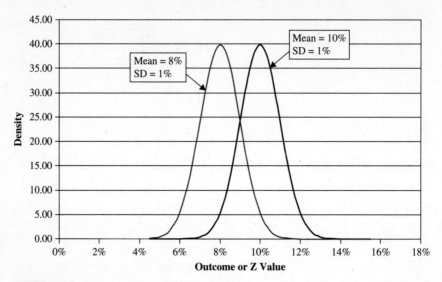

FIGURE 2.4B Shifting the Normal Distribution

function documents that the curve describes how observations are clustered somewhat densely around the mean. Observations farther and farther from the mean become less common (as shown by the vanishing bell shapes to the right and left of the mean). The outcome is displayed on the X or horizontal axis of Figures 2.4A and 2.4B, while the likelihood of each of these outcomes is displayed on the Y or vertical axis. Notice that the highest values on the vertical axis occur at the center of the bell shape and other outcomes (values to the left or right on the X axis) are less likely. This lower likelihood explains the lower values on the Y axis for these outcomes and creates the bell-like shape for the normal curve.

To make things clearer, think about the normal distribution as a probability curve. Outcomes near the mean are likely to occur and outcomes far from the mean occur infrequently at best. The area under the curve in Figure 2.4A (and bounded by the bottom graph axis) represents all possible outcomes. You can visually confirm (based on the size of the regions under the curve) that an observation above 10 percent is about equally as likely as an observation below 10 percent. It also appears that falling within the range of 9 percent to 11 percent (on the X axis) happens about two-thirds of the time. It also appears that an observation would be greater than 11.5 percent only about 5 percent of the time.

The curve in Figure 2.4A is the same curve as the taller curve in Figure 2.4C, with a mean of 10 percent and a standard deviation of 1 percent. The shorter curve in Figure 2.4C also has a mean of 10 percent but a standard

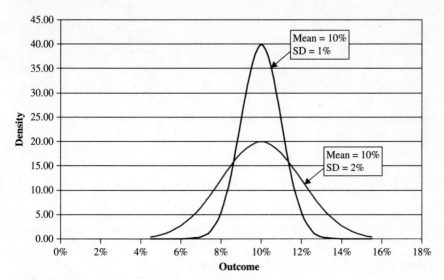

FIGURE 2.4C Normal Distribution—Different Volatility

deviation of 2 percent. While it is still true that half of the observations are above or below 10 percent, a bit more than one-third of the observations are between 9 percent and 11 percent. In addition, over 5 percent of the observations are greater than 13.25 percent.

The standard deviation is used to adapt the normal distribution to more or less volatile data series. In fact, the standard deviation is often called *volatility* in option pricing. The normal distribution (as configured with the mean and standard deviation) is used to estimate probabilities of outcomes for Monte Carlo simulations and in other areas where a measure of uncertain is part of the analysis.

THE CUMULATIVE DENSITY FUNCTION

The familiar bell curve or normal distribution underlies much of the statistics used in finance and investments. However, one adjustment is often necessary. As mentioned previously, the normal distribution is a probability function. However, it is frequently necessary to know the probability of an occurrence within a range. For example, if expected returns equal 10 percent and the standard deviation of return is 1 percent, what is the likelihood that the return will be between 9 percent and 11 percent?

A useful tool is the cumulative probability under a normal curve. In Figure 2.4A, notice that the curve is centered on 10 percent and the left and

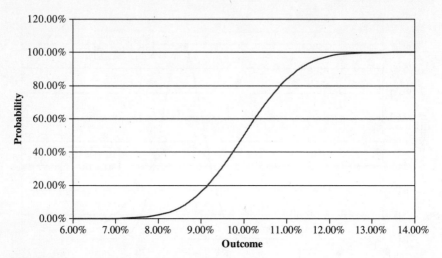

FIGURE 2.5   Cumulative Normal Distribution

right sides are symmetric. As a result, it is correct (and intuitive) to conclude that half of the time the returns for this asset are above 10 percent and half of the time they are below 10 percent.

To generalize this point, review Equation 2.7. This equation allows computers to generate the normal curve for any set of inputs. If you input the mean, standard deviation, and a data point (x), it is possible to generate a point on the normal curve for that set of inputs. The cumulative normal distribution describes, for a particular value of x, the probability that the actual return will equal that value or less. For example, the probability of observing a return of 10 percent or less when the mean return is 10 percent does in fact equal 50 percent, as can be visually confirmed in Figure 2.5, which shows the cumulative probability of the outcomes previously presented in Figure 2.4A.

Table 2.4 is a list of cumulative probabilities used to construct Figure 2.5.

From Table 2.4, it is possible to determine the probability that the return will range between 9 percent and 11 percent. We observe that 84.13 percent of the time, the return is 11 percent or less. We also note that 15.87 percent of the time, the return is 9 percent or less. Therefore, the probability that the return is between 9 percent and 11 percent is 84.13% − 15.87% = 68.27%.

MEASURES OF DEPENDENCY

As you observe two data series (for example, the returns on two investments), it is often important to measure the extent to which one outcome

TABLE 2.4 Cumulative Normal Distribution

Return	Probability
6.00%	0.00%
6.50%	0.02%
7.00%	0.13%
7.50%	0.62%
8.00%	2.28%
8.50%	6.68%
9.00%	15.87%
9.50%	30.85%
10.00%	50.00%
10.50%	69.15%
11.00%	84.13%
11.50%	93.32%
12.00%	97.72%
12.50%	99.38%
13.00%	99.87%
13.50%	99.98%
14.00%	100.00%

generally tracks another. For example, in Figure 2.6 the returns on two securities track each other closely. If the return on Asset 1 is above average (if the return is plotted to the right of the bar depicting the average return for Asset 1), it is quite likely that the return on Asset 2 will be above average (plotted above the bar depicting the average return for Asset 2).

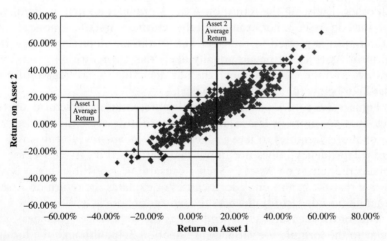

FIGURE 2.6 Covariance and Correlation High

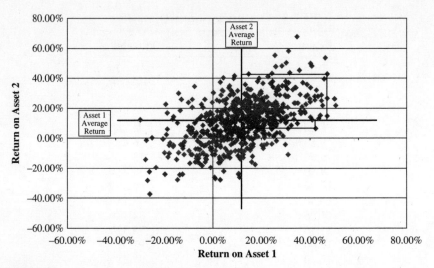

FIGURE 2.7 Covariance and Correlation Moderate

The returns on the two assets in Figure 2.7 do not track each other as closely. Nevertheless, there is still a tendency for high returns to occur together on the two investments. For example, if the return on Asset 1 is above average (if the return is plotted to the right half of the bar depicting the average return for Asset 1), it is still somewhat more likely than not that the return on Asset 2 will be above average (plotted above the bar depicting the average return for Asset 2).

Finally, the two investments in Figure 2.8 are virtually independent of each other. Knowing the return on Asset 1 provides no help in predicting the return on Asset 2. For example, if the return on Asset 1 is above average (if the return is plotted to the right half of the bar depicting the average return for Asset 1), it appears equally likely that the return on Asset 2 will be above average (plotted above the bar depicting the average return for Asset 2) or below (plotted below the bar).

Figures 2.6 to 2.8 provide a visual representation of returns on two assets that are more or less related. Statisticians describe this tendency of two or more variables to move together as *dependency*. In this case, the word "dependency" does not imply that the return on Asset 1 causes or explains the return on Asset 2. Such a causal link is possible, but it is also possible that the return on Asset 2 causes or explains the return on Asset 1 or that an outside factor influences the returns of both assets.

One of the measures of dependency is the covariance. This measure is similar to the formula for variance in Equation 2.4b, although the formula

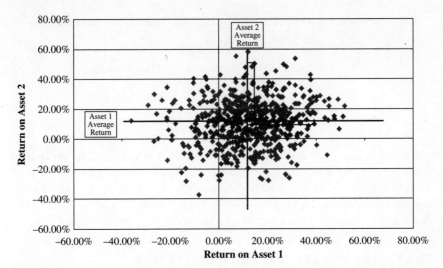

FIGURE 2.8 Covariance and Correlation Low

in Equation 2.8 has been extended to two variables.

$$\sigma_{r1,r2} = \frac{\sum (r_1 - \bar{r}_1)(r_2 - \bar{r}_2)}{N - 1} \qquad (2.8)$$

The symbol sigma ($\sigma_{r1,r2}$), which is used to represent standard deviation (σ) and variance (σ^2), is also used here to represent the covariance. However, the same symbol applied to the standard deviation and variance has at most one subscript (e.g., σ_{r1} or σ_{r1}^2, although this subscript is frequently omitted when it is not needed to prevent confusion), whereas the symbol for covariance has two subscripts, documenting the dependency between these two variables. Also, the symbol for covariance has no superscript.

Notice, too, that if the covariance is calculated on one series of data (in other words, the data in $r2$ is actually the $r1$ data), this formula becomes exactly the formula for variance in Equation 2.4b.

A second measure of dependency is called correlation, usually represented by the Greek letter rho (ρ). Like the covariance, the correlation is calculated with two data series. For this reason, the correlation is sometimes shown with two subscripts, representing the two data series used to calculate the correlation. For example, $\rho_{r1,r2}$ would represent the correlation between rates r_1 and r_2.

The formula for correlation in Equations 2.9a and 2.9b is as follows:

$$\text{Correlation}_{r1,r2} = \frac{\text{Covariance}_{r1,r2}}{\text{Standard deviation}_{r1} * \text{Standard deviation}_{r2}} \quad (2.9a)$$

$$\rho_{r1,r2} = \frac{\sigma_{r1,r2}}{\sigma_{r1}\sigma_{r2}} \quad (2.9b)$$

Correlation ranges from a maximum value of 1 (the two variables move completely in lockstep) to zero (the two variables move independently of each other) to –1 (the two variables move in lockstep in opposite directions). The correlation between the return on Asset 1 and the return on Asset 2 was .90 for Figure 2.6, .50 for Figure 2.7, and .00 for Figure 2.8.

MEASURING COVARIANCE AND CORRELATION

Table 2.5 presents two series of data that are statistically related. The first data series in the far-left column is drawn from a population with a mean of 10 percent and a standard deviation of 1 percent. The second series in the third column is drawn from a population with a mean of 9 percent and a standard deviation of 2 percent.

TABLE 2.5   Calculating Covariance

	Asset 1	Deviation	Asset 2	Deviation	Product
	11.051%	1.053%	10.571%	1.559%	0.016%
	9.604%	−0.394%	7.381%	−1.631%	0.006%
	8.315%	−1.683%	6.005%	−3.007%	0.051%
	10.088%	0.090%	10.421%	1.409%	0.001%
	10.376%	0.378%	11.408%	2.396%	0.009%
	8.732%	−1.267%	8.796%	−0.217%	0.003%
	10.004%	0.006%	8.662%	−0.350%	0.000%
	10.048%	0.050%	5.844%	−3.168%	−0.002%
	11.375%	1.375%	9.286%	0.274%	0.004%
	10.389%	0.391%	11.750%	2.737%	0.011%
Sum	99.984%	0.000%	90.124%	0.000%	0.099%
Mean	9.998%	0.000%	9.012%	0.000%	0.010%
Standard Deviation	0.937%		2.099%		
				Covariance	0.00011
				Correlation	0.5617

The first step is to calculate the mean returns for each series. The returns on the first asset average 9.998 percent, or approximately 10 percent. The returns on the second asset average 9.012 percent, or just over 9 percent. The standard deviation for each asset was calculated following the procedure used in Table 2.3, applying Equation 2.5b. The deviations from the mean are calculated for each asset, following the same procedure used in Table 2.3. Now, however, the two deviations are multiplied together in the column labeled Product. The sum of these deviations as displayed in the far-right column equals the numerator in Equation 2.8. The covariance is this sum divided by the number of observations (here, 10) less 1.

The correlation equals the covariance calculated as described, divided by the standard deviation of Asset 1 and that of Asset 2. For the returns listed on Table 2.5, the correlation equals the covariance of .00011, divided by the standard deviation of 0.937 for Asset 1 and 2.099 for Asset 2, or .5617.

The means, standard deviations, and correlations of the sampled returns for the two assets used in this example match the population statistics fairly closely. For samples of 10 returns, the mean, standard deviation, and correlation may differ significantly from the population. In practice, a sample should be large enough to provide a reliable estimate of the population statistics.

CALCULATING STATISTICS IN PRACTICE

The examples in Table 2.3 and Table 2.5 allow the reader to understand how the statistics in this chapter are calculated. In practice, most of the time it is possible to rely on routines that calculate these values from the data with efficient and accurate built-in routines. For example, Excel has built-in functions that calculate the mean, median, variance, standard deviation, covariance, and correlation. These functions are accurate for most applications. Other software (e.g., SAS, SPSS, Matlab, Mathmatica, and some programming languages) also has built-in functions to calculate popular statistics.

The questions and answers following this chapter will provide an opportunity to use the Excel routines to calculate the statistics described in this chapter. See the answers at the back of the book for examples of some Excel tools being used for statistical analysis.

COMBINING NORMAL DISTRIBUTIONS

It is possible to predict the mean and standard deviation of a combination of two or more normal distributions (either adding two or more separate

	A	B	C	D
Expected Return	12.00%	11.00%	10.00%	9.00%
Standard Deviation	15.00%	14.00%	13.00%	12.00%

FIGURE 2.9   Expect Risk and Returns

variables or subtracting one variable from another). Consider a four-stock portfolio. All of the stocks are correlated to the others to greater or lesser degrees. Each stock has a different expected return and expected volatility of return.

Figure 2.9 shows the expected return and standard deviation for each stock.

Figure 2.10 shows the expected correlation between the individual stocks.

By definition, Stock A always moves in perfect alignment with Stock A (correlation is 1 or 100 percent). Similarly, all the diagonal elements are perfectly correlated as shown in boldface.

Note that the upper-right diagonal half of the table exactly matches the lower-left part of the table. The correlation of Stock A with Stock D is identical to the correlation of Stock D with Stock A. For this reason, the shaded part of the table is often omitted.

From the information in Figures 2.9 and 2.10, it is possible to fill out the diagonal members of the variance–covariance matrix. The diagonal elements are the variances of the individual stocks. The variance of Stock A is the square of the standard deviation of Stock A (15 percent ∗ 15 percent = 2.25 percent). (See Figure 2.11A.)

Similarly, the variance of Stock B is 14 percent ∗ 14 percent, or 1.96 percent. The variance of Stock C is 13 percent ∗ 13 percent, or 1.69 percent, and the variance of Stock D is 12 percent ∗ 12 percent, or 1.44 percent. The covariances in Figure 2.11A can be filled in with the help of Equation 2.10, which follows. Begin with the formula for correlation (Equation 2.9a).

	A	B	C	D
A	**1.00**	0.75	0.65	0.55
B	0.75	**1.00**	0.45	0.35
C	0.65	0.45	**1.00**	0.25
D	0.55	0.35	0.25	**1.00**

FIGURE 2.10   Correlation Matrix

	A	B	C	D
A	2.25%			
B		1.96%		
C			1.69%	
D				1.44%

FIGURE 2.11A   Variance–Covariance Matrix

$$\text{Correlation}_{r1,r2} = \frac{\text{Covariance}_{r1,r2}}{\text{Standard deviation}_{r1} * \text{Standard deviation}_{r2}}$$

(repeating Equation 2.9a)

Therefore, rearranging terms, the covariance between two data series can be determined from the correlation between the two series and the standard deviation of each series.

$$\text{Covariance}_{r1,r2} = \text{Correlation}_{r1,r2} * \text{Standard deviation}_{r1} * \text{Standard deviation}_{r2}$$

(2.10)

For example, the covariance between Stock A and Stock B is equal to the correlation between Stock A and Stock B times the standard deviation of both Stock A and Stock B (.75 * 15 percent * 14 percent, or 1.58 percent). Similarly, the covariance between Stock A and Stock C is .65 * 15 percent * 13 percent, or 1.27 percent.

The variances from Figure 2.11A have been carried over in boldface onto Figure 2.11B. Each of the covariance terms was calculated as described in the preceding text and in Equation 2.9 and appears in the lower-right corner of the variance–covariance table. The upper-right diagonal half of the table is identical to the lower-right portion and is often not displayed.

Suppose the portfolio contains equal dollar investments in the four stocks. Figure 2.12 documents that assumption.

	A	B	C	D
A	**2.25%**	1.58%	1.27%	0.99%
B	1.58%	**1.96%**	0.82%	0.59%
C	1.27%	0.82%	**1.69%**	0.39%
D	0.99%	0.59%	0.39%	**1.44%**

FIGURE 2.11B   Variance–Covariance Matrix

A	B	C	D
25%	25%	25%	25%

FIGURE 2.12 Portfolio Weights

A	B	C	D	Combined
3.00%	2.75%	2.50%	2.25%	10.50%

FIGURE 2.13 Portfolio Returns

The combined effect of these weights and the expected return is shown in Figure 2.13. If 25 percent of the portfolio is invested in Stock A, which returns 12 percent, that return contributes 3 percent (25 percent $*$ 12 percent) to the portfolio return. The portfolio also expects to make 11 percent on 25 percent of the portfolio invested in Stock B, contributing 2.75 percent. Similarly, Stock C is expected to contribute 2.5 percent (10 percent $*$ 25 percent) and Stock D contributes 2.25 percent (25 percent $*$ 9 percent).

$$\text{Return}_{\text{Portfolio}} = \text{Return}_A * w_A + \text{Return}_B * w_B \qquad (2.11)$$

The expected return of the portfolio is equal to a straightforward combination of the individual expected returns (as shown in Equation 2.11). If the returns of two assets are combined, Equation 2.11 describes the method used to create a combined or portfolio return. If the portfolio contains more assets, then more returns and weights must be used to calculate the portfolio return.

It is also possible to calculate the variance or standard deviation of the portfolio from the variance or standard deviation of the components of the portfolio. The formula for the standard deviation of a two-asset portfolio is shown in Equation 2.12. The more general case is shown in Equation 2.13. For N variables and weight w_1 to w_N:

$$\sigma_{\text{Portfolio}} = \sqrt{w_A^2 \sigma_A^2 + 2 w_A w_B \sigma_{A,B} + w_B^2 \sigma_B^2} \qquad (2.12)$$

$$\sigma_{\text{Portfolio}} = \sqrt{\sum_{i=1}^{N} \sum_{j=1}^{N} w_i w_j \sigma_{i,j}} \qquad (2.13)$$

The formula in Equation 2.13 calls for applying weights to all the 16 elements in the variance–covariance table in Figure 2.11B. For consistency

	A	B	C	D
A	6.25%	6.25%	6.25%	6.25%
B	6.25%	6.25%	6.25%	6.25%
C	6.25%	6.25%	6.25%	6.25%
D	6.25%	6.25%	6.25%	6.25%

FIGURE 2.14 Weights for Equation 2.12

(and easy calculation in a spreadsheet), Figure 2.14 contains the weights for each of these 16 variances and covariances.

The weights in Figure 2.14 are all equal because the stocks in the portfolio are equally weighted. In the more general case, Figure 2.14 could contain various combined weights.

Figure 2.15 contains each of the calculations for each pass through the formula in Equation 2.13, maintained in the same table format as the original variance–covariance matrix.

For example, the first pass through Equation 2.13 combines the weight on Stock A with the weight on Stock A times the covariance (i.e., variance) on Stock A (2.25 percent * 25 percent * 25 percent, or 0.00141) and appears on the upper-left cell on Figure 2.15. The second pass through the table combines the weight on Stock A, the weight on Stock B, and the covariance between Stock A and Stock B (25 percent * 25 percent * 1.47 percent, or 0.00092). Note that this same calculation appears twice in Figure 2.15 in the cells immediately to the right and immediately below the upper-left cell.

Each of these 16 items in Figure 2.15 contributes to the risk of the portfolio. The sum of the 16 items is the variance of the portfolio, in this case 1.162 percent. The standard deviation is the square root of this variance, or 10.78 percent. Notice that the standard deviation of the portfolio is lower than the standard deviation of any of the individual stocks in the portfolio.

	A	B	C	D
A	0.00141	0.00098	0.00079	0.00062
B	0.00098	0.00123	0.00051	0.00037
C	0.00079	0.00051	0.00106	0.00024
D	0.00062	0.00037	0.00024	0.00090

FIGURE 2.15 Formula Elements

CONCLUSION

Finance relies heavily on the statistical characteristics of returns. Later chapters in this book discuss how risk, as measured by some of the tools presented in this chapter, determines the required return on an investment. These tools can also be used to value investments for which the size and timing of returns is uncertain.

Use the following sample data to answer the questions in Chapter 2:

Return	Rank
9.70%	5
11.50%	10
8.40%	2
8.40%	3
10.90%	8
10.20%	6
9.20%	4
11.00%	9
8.30%	1
10.40%	7

2.1. What is the median return in the table of sample data?

2.2. What is the mean or average return of the 10 returns in the sample data?

2.3. What is the variance of the sample data?

2.4. What is the standard deviation of the returns in sample data?

2.5. You are considering investing in a project. Your engineering department has reviewed many factors that could affect the profitability of the project and reports that the project should have an expected profit (as measured by your accountants) of $300,000 per year. Those factors create considerable uncertainty. The engineers believe that the actual profit is normally distributed with a standard deviation of $250,000. The CEO admits that this information is not helpful to him and asks how likely the project is to break even or lose money? Can you answer the CEO's question?

2.6. Suppose a different project has an expected return of $500,000 and an estimated standard deviation of $500,000. What is the probability of loss for this project?

2.7. Does the probability of default provide a basis for comparing the two projects?

2.8. Suppose that the company can invest an equal amount in both of the projects in Questions 2.5–2.6. Further, the correlation of returns is .40. What is the mean net income and the standard deviation?

2.9. Suppose that you can invest in a number of projects and the return on each of the projects is completely uncorrelated. What can you say about the standard deviation of the portfolio?

2.10. Use the data that follows to calculate the beta for IBM versus the S&P 500. Ignore dividends and assume that the risk-free rate is 5 percent.

Closing Prices for S&P 500 and IBM

Date	S&P 500	IBM
12/29/2006	1,418.30	93.16
1/31/2007	1,438.24	95.08
2/28/2007	1,406.82	89.39
3/30/2007	1,420.86	90.66
4/30/2007	1,482.37	98.31
5/31/2007	1,530.62	102.93
6/29/2007	1,503.35	101.62
7/31/2007	1,455.27	106.84
8/31/2007	1,473.99	113.07
9/28/2007	1,526.75	114.14
10/31/2007	1,549.38	112.52
11/30/2007	1,481.14	102.28
12/31/2007	1,468.36	105.12

2.11. What is the alpha of IBM using the foregoing prices for IBM and the S&P 500 for 2007?

CHAPTER 3

Core Finance Theories and the Cost of Capital

INTRODUCTION

This chapter presents several important theories that provide a basis for assessing risk and determining what rate to use in valuing cash flows with the tools presented in Chapter 1. In addition, it briefly discusses how to determine the proportion of debt and equity a company should use and how to determine the dividend that will result in the highest stock price.

RISK REDUCTION FROM DIVERSIFICATION

Equations 2.12 and 2.13 in Chapter 2 document how the standard deviation of a portfolio depends on the standard deviation of the individual assets in the portfolio as well as the dependencies between the returns of the assets in the portfolio. Equation 3.1 repeats the formula for the standard deviation of a portfolio (listed earlier as Equation 2.13).

$$\sigma_{\text{Portfolio}} = \sqrt{\sum_{i=1}^{N} \sum_{j=1}^{N} w_i \, w_j \, \sigma_{i,j}} \qquad (3.1)$$

Table 3.1 lists a variance-covariance matrix values for four stocks. The returns on each of the stocks were assumed to have a standard deviation equal to 20 percent, and the correlation of the stocks equals .50 between all stocks in the portfolio. Although the standard deviations and correlations of actual stocks are not so consistent, the table nevertheless demonstrates the impact of diversification on portfolio risk as measured by standard deviation.

TABLE 3.1 Variance-Covariance Matrix

	Stock 1	Stock 2	Stock 3	Stock 4
Stock 1	**4.00%**	2.00%	2.00%	2.00%
Stock 2	2.00%	**4.00%**	2.00%	2.00%
Stock 3	2.00%	2.00%	**4.00%**	2.00%
Stock 4	2.00%	2.00%	2.00%	**4.00%**

The covariance of Stock 1 return with Stock 1 return is equal to the variance of the Stock 1 return. Therefore, this value equals the square of the standard deviation of 20 percent or 4 percent. The variances of each stock are shown in boldface in Table 3.1.

The covariance of the return on Stock 1 to the return on Stock 2 equals the correlation of the return on Stock 1 to the return on Stock 2 times the standard deviation of the return on Stock 1 times the standard deviation of return on Stock 2. This relationship is documented by Equation 2.10 in Chapter 2. This covariance is therefore .50 * 20 percent * 20 percent or 2 percent. Because, in this example, the correlations between all stock returns equal .50 and because the standard deviation of each stock return equals 20 percent, each of the remaining elements of the variance covariance matrix also equals 2 percent.

In each of the following sample portfolios, hypothetical positions of increasing numbers of individual stocks were equally weighted. A single-stock portfolio puts 100 percent of the assets in one stock. A two-stock portfolio uses weights of 50 percent in each stock. A three-stock portfolio puts 33.3 percent in each stock. This weighting scheme continues for portfolios containing more stocks.

Table 3.2 lists the standard deviation of a portfolio composed of one or more stocks and measures the impact of diversification on the risk of the portfolio.

The reduction in portfolio standard deviation diminishes as the number of stocks included in the portfolios on Table 3.2 increases. The addition of the second stock contributes toward a greater than 10 percent reduction in risk. Each additional stock, however, reduces risk by a diminished amount. As a result, most of the benefits of diversification in this equally weighted hypothetical portfolio occur before the size of the portfolio reaches 10 stocks. Many investment professionals believe that most of the benefits of diversification (not necessarily equally weighted) are present in a portfolio of 20 actual stocks.

Figure 3.1 shows the benefits of diversification graphically. Figure 3.1 plots the standard deviation of return for portfolios of 1 to 25 stocks as

TABLE 3.2 Portfolio Standard Deviation of Return

Stocks	Weight	Standard Deviation
1	100%	20.00%
2	50%	17.32%
3	33%	16.33%
4	25%	15.81%
5	20%	15.49%
10	10%	14.83%
20	5%	14.49%
100	1%	14.21%

constructed for Table 3.2. Two important points are made visually in Figure 3.1 First, diversification is a powerful risk-reducing tool and can have a major impact on the risk faced by investors. Second, diversification cannot eliminate all risk for most assets.

For stock returns that are highly correlated (near 1.00), diversification can eliminate very little portfolio risk. For stock returns that are not highly correlated (near 0.00 or below), diversification can eliminate a substantial amount of risk. In practice, the returns on stocks in most portfolios are correlated and diversification cannot eliminate all risk.

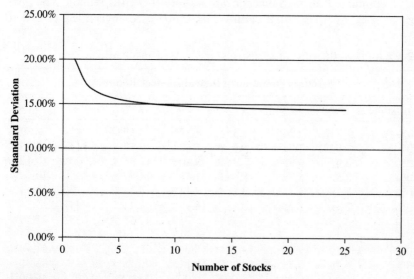

FIGURE 3.1 Adding Stocks Improves Diversification

One important theory that follows from an understanding of the power and limits of diversification is that investors will demand to be compensated for risks that they cannot diversify away, but they will not be paid for risks that can be removed by diversification.

SYSTEMATIC VERSUS UNSYSTEMATIC RISK

Table 3.3 highlights the benefits and limits of diversification. The table lists a range of standard deviations from left to right, representing the riskiness of individual stocks. A standard deviation of return of 5 percent is more stable than a typical stock under most market conditions. Individual stock return volatility higher than 35 percent is common for technology companies and young, fast-growing companies.

The correlation of individual stock returns in Table 3.3 ranges from 0 percent to 100 percent. Note that correlations can be negative; negative correlations are not included in Table 3.3, however, because such correlations are not common.

Notice that, for a 20-stock portfolio, the portfolio does not completely diversify away risk even for stocks that are completely uncorrelated. Notice, too, that, if stock returns are perfectly correlated, diversification provides no risk reduction.

Under most market conditions, some part of an individual stock return can be eliminated through diversification, but other risks remain. The portion of a company's stock return that cannot be diversified is called

TABLE 3.3   Diversification of a 20-Stock Equally Weighted Portfolio

Correlation	Standard Deviation of Individual Stock Return						
	5%	10%	15%	20%	25%	30%	35%
0%	1.12%	2.24%	3.35%	4.47%	5.59%	6.71%	7.83%
10%	1.90%	3.81%	5.71%	7.62%	9.52%	11.42%	13.33%
20%	2.45%	4.90%	7.35%	9.80%	12.25%	14.70%	17.15%
30%	2.89%	5.79%	8.68%	11.58%	14.47%	17.36%	20.26%
40%	3.28%	6.56%	9.84%	13.11%	16.39%	19.67%	22.95%
50%	3.62%	7.25%	10.87%	14.49%	18.11%	21.74%	25.36%
60%	3.94%	7.87%	11.81%	15.75%	19.69%	23.62%	27.56%
70%	4.23%	8.46%	12.68%	16.91%	21.14%	25.37%	29.60%
80%	4.50%	9.00%	13.50%	18.00%	22.50%	27.00%	31.50%
90%	4.76%	9.51%	14.27%	19.03%	23.78%	28.54%	33.30%
100%	5.00%	10.00%	15.00%	20.00%	25.00%	30.00%	35.00%

systematic risk. The portion of the company's stock return that can be diversified away is called unsystematic risk.

THE MARKET PORTFOLIO

Because diversification can eliminate unsystematic risk, investors should seek to reduce as much unsystematic risk as possible. Financial theory holds that the best possible diversification occurs when all conceivable assets are merged into a single portfolio. No investor could buy all assets in the marketplace for many practical reasons. However, as a standard for pricing, it is convenient to assume that an investor could completely diversify away unsystematic risk.

The definition of the market portfolio is ambiguous. However, the market portfolio is more diversified than popular market indices such as the Dow Jones Industrial Average or the Standard & Poor's 500 Index. The market portfolio should also include small stocks, corporate bonds, mortgage investments, real estate, venture capital, and international investments.

In fact, many investment professionals specialize in creating and marketing nonstandard assets, such as private equity and hedge funds. One of the strongest arguments favoring investments in illiquid and sometimes very risky assets is that these assets are weakly correlated to broadly diversified stock and bond returns. By including these so-called alternative assets in a portfolio, investors may be able to improve the diversification of their portfolios.

THE CAPITAL ASSET PRICING MODEL

The Capital Asset Pricing Model (CAPM) proposes a way that the market accounts for the undiversifiable or systematic risk in a portfolio. According to this theory, investors are not compensated for risks that can be diversified. The risk that cannot be diversified is the market return.

The model begins with the belief that there are two efficient assets. One asset is risk free and provides a low rate of return. This risk-free asset should be free of default risk and sensitivity to market pricing. Investors and academics usually use either the return on U.S. Treasury bills or the Libor bank lending rate as the rate of return on risk-free assets. The second efficient asset that an investor might hold is the market portfolio. The expected return on the market portfolio compensates investors for a risk premium above the risk-free rate to compensate for systematic risk. The expected return does not compensate for diversifiable risk because the market portfolio has diversified away as much unsystematic (diversifiable) risk as possible.

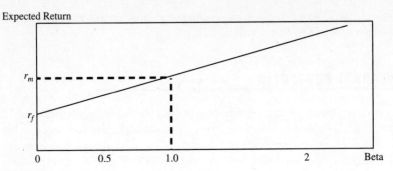

FIGURE 3.2 Security Market Line

Investors get the maximum amount of risk reduction if they invest in only risk-free assets and the market portfolio. Investors who want to avoid all risk should invest all of their money in risk-free assets. Investors who tolerate risk well might invest all of their money in the market portfolio. Investors with a modest tolerance for risk could invest some of their money in risk-free assets and some in the market portfolio.

Figure 3.2 depicts the Security Market Line. Investors can achieve any point on the line connecting the risk-free rate and the expected market return by changing the portion of their assets invested in risk-free assets and the market portfolio. If investors can borrow money at the risk-free rate, they can increase their returns along the same line by leveraging the market portfolio.

The measure of risk on the horizontal axis is beta. Beta is defined as the covariance of a particular stock divided by the variance of expected market return.

$$\beta_i = \frac{\sigma_{i,m}}{\sigma_m^2} \tag{3.2}$$

The expected return of a particular stock (r_i) depends on the risk-free rate (labeled r_f in Equation 3.3), the expected return for the market portfolio (labeled r_m in Equation 3.3), and beta (β_i). The risk premium for a particular stock is calculated as shown in Equation 3.3.

$$r_i - r_f = \beta_i(r_m - r_f) \tag{3.3}$$

This beta is the same statistic found in the regression section of a statistical textbook. In fact, one way to calculate the beta of a stock would be to run a regression using the return on the individual stock as the dependent variable and the return on the market as the independent variable.

When viewed as a regression statistic, the meaning of beta is clear. If an individual stock has a beta equal to 2, the expected return in excess of the risk-free rate—the risk premium for the individual stock—would be double the risk premium for the market. Stocks that have a beta equal to 1 have no more or less systematic risk than the market portfolio. Stocks that have a beta larger than 1 have a concentrated portion of systematic risk and contribute more than proportionately to the risk in a diversified portfolio. Stocks that have a beta smaller than one have a diluted portion of systematic risk and contribute less than proportionately to the risk in a diversified portfolio.

USING BETA TO DETERMINE THE REQUIRED RETURN FOR A STOCK

In Chapter 1, cash flows were discounted at various rates as present value and future value tools were introduced. At one point, it was suggested that the appropriate rate might be a bank lending rate. That lending rate would be appropriate only if it properly accounted for the systematic or undiversifiable risk of the underlying cash flows.

If Equation 3.3 is slightly rearranged, CAPM can be used to determine an appropriate discount rate for an asset, a new capital investment, or any series of cash flows. Equation 3.4 adjusts the market risk premium up by beta then adds back the risk-free rate.

$$r_i = \beta_i(r_m - r_f) + r_f \qquad (3.4)$$

CAPM provides a way to determine the return required by the shareholders. This return is also called the equity cost of capital. Equation 3.5 will show how companies use this required return to determine the rate used for making investment decisions.

OTHER FACTOR MODELS

The Capital Asset Pricing Model assumes that risk can be completely described as the undiversifiable portion of risk and that risk can be defined as the standard deviation of return. The Arbitrage Pricing Theory (APT) posits that the required return cannot be adequately described in terms of undiversifiable risk. Instead, the returns should depend on short-term interest rates, the difference between short- and long-term rates, currency markets, inflation, and real economic growth. To use the APT or to add other risk factors, it is necessary to measure the sensitivity of stock returns to each of the identified factors. The result is a more complicated but potentially more accurate way to determine the required return on a stock.

COST OF DEBT

Some companies issue debt frequently. These companies can easily determine the cost of borrowed money. That cost should include underwriting fees and other charges. The cost of debt borrowing should also include the tax savings from the deduction of interest expense from taxable corporate income. In Chapter 1, Equations 1.28 and 1.29 used the after-tax cost of debt financing to determine present and future value.

Companies that do not issue debt regularly may be able to determine their cost of debt from the pricing of their outstanding debt issues. For example, if a company had previously issued debt with a 5 percent coupon that now trades at a discount, the company's current cost of debt would be above 5 percent. Equation 4.13 in the following chapter values such a bond when the required return had risen from 5 percent to 6 percent. The same pricing tools could be used to determine the appropriate interest rate for a company at any point in time.

Some companies have not issued debt. If it is possible to identify one or more companies that are similar and that have issued debt, it may be possible to determine an appropriate cost of debt from these comparable companies.

WEIGHTED AVERAGE COST OF CAPITAL

Companies may finance their operations with a blend of debt and equity. A company considering a capital investment may choose to finance that particular project with cash on hand, new debt financing, or retained earnings (equity) or through a new stock offering. Each of the alternatives would suggest a different discount rate to use for present value and future value calculations.

Present value and future value calculations should not depend on short-term incremental decisions about funding. For various reasons, companies often maintain a nearly constant mix of debt and equity. For these companies, a weighted average cost of capital (WACC) could include the present weights of debt and equity. For a company that plans to change its capital structure in the direction of more debt or more equity, it may be appropriate to use these target weightings.

The weighted average cost of capital is described in Equation 3.5.

$$\text{WACC} = \frac{\text{Debt}}{\text{Debt} + \text{Equity}} R_{\text{Debt}}(1 - \text{Tax}) + \frac{\text{Equity}}{\text{Debt} + \text{Equity}} R_{\text{Equity}} \quad (3.5)$$

The first part of the equation (debt divided by total capital) is the weight of debt in the capital structure. This weight is multiplied by the cost of debt adjusted downward to account for the tax savings the company receives by deducting interest payments on the corporate tax return. The second part of the equation (equity divided by total capital) is the weight of equity in the capital structure. This weight is multiplied by the equity cost of capital.

For example, suppose Albatross Manufacturing could borrow at 9 percent before tax savings. The company pays corporate taxes at a 35 percent marginal rate. The company's equity cost of capital is 13.5 percent. Finally, the company has $200 million in debt outstanding (current value) and $300 million equity. The company's WACC is

$$\text{WACC} = \frac{200}{200 + 300} 9.00\%(1 - 35\%) + \frac{300}{200 + 300} 13.5\%$$
$$= 10.44\% \quad (3.6)$$

If Albatross needs to do present value or future value calculations, it would probably use a discount rate close to 10.44 percent. Chapter 4 introduces several techniques that Albatross could use to evaluate new investments. These tools require the user to know the discount rate that is appropriate for the company considering market conditions and the riskiness of the business and its investments.

MODIGLIANI AND MILLER

The mix of debt and equity (leverage) in the capital structure is necessary to calculate the weighted average cost of capital. Of course, companies must determine the mix of capital. Franco Modigliani and Merton Miller showed that in a hypothetical world without taxes and with no cost of bankruptcy, a company should not be able to increase the value of the firm by changing its mix of debt and equity. If the leverage changed, the bond holders and the stock holders would require more or less of the total return commensurate with the risks for their investment, but the total value of the firm would not be affected by leverage decisions.

In the real world, in which corporations can deduct interest, the tax savings motivates corporate treasurers to include more debt in their capital structure than if the tax subsidy did not exist. As can be seen in Equations 3.5 and 3.6, the after-tax cost of debt is lower because of tax savings. Lowering the cost of debt also lowers the weighted average cost of capital. Chapter 4 shows that lowering a company's cost of capital can increase the company's value and permit the company to profitably invest in projects that it otherwise might reject.

Increasing the debt too much can significantly raise the chance of bankruptcy. Bankruptcy is expensive in several respects. The out-of-pocket cost of bankruptcy is high, because the legal process is expensive. The cost to workers and managers who might lose their jobs is high. For these reasons, corporate treasurers are constrained in the amount of debt they can add to a company's balance sheet.

PATTERNS OF DEBT AND EQUITY IN CAPITAL STRUCTURES

Companies have an incentive to use more debt in a company's capital structure because tax deductibility reduces the cost of debt but not the cost of equity. Nevertheless, companies still use equity in their capital structure. A pattern often develops concerning the use of debt and equity. Fast-growing technology companies generally use little or no debt. Capital-intensive industries, such as industrial manufacturing, public utilities, and airlines, typically rely heavily on debt financing. Risks, growth, profitability, cyclicality, and a number of other factors determine the amount of debt used by individual companies. Within sectors, individual companies often make similar decisions about how much debt to use.

Debt and equity usage varies substantially from company to company, but leverage for a particular company varies much less over time. As a result, the use of existing weights to determine WACC has become acceptable for most companies.

CONCLUSION

The Capital Asset Pricing Model provides a method for determining the equity cost of capital for a company. The market for corporate bonds provides a way to identify the cost of debt for a company. Financial models rely on these key inputs to make investment decisions, as described in Chapter 4.

3.1. Your company can issue new debt at 8.15 percent (including all issuing costs and fees). The company's marginal tax rate is 35 percent. What is the after-tax cost of debt capital for the company?

3.2. Your company has a pretax cost of debt of 8.15 percent, an equity cost of capital of 12 percent and a corporate tax rate of 35 percent. The company's debt-to-equity ratio is .6, and it plans to maintain that ratio. What is the firm's weighted average cost of capital (WACC)?

3.3. Using the information in Question 3.2, what is the company's average return on assets?

CHAPTER 4

Capital Budgeting Tools

INTRODUCTION

The time value of money tools presented in Chapter 1 provide a methodology for evaluating business investments. Chapter 1 applied the tools to an individual cash flow. More often, investments are made over a period of time, and the returns arrive at several times. It takes just a simple extension of the present value/future value analysis to be able to evaluate complex projects.

THREE WAYS TO EVALUATE INVESTMENTS

The simplest investment involves an immediate investment or cash outflow and a return of a (hopefully) larger cash inflow at a later time. The tools introduced in Chapter 1 provide a basis for judging the merits of this investment.

The first method, called the payback method, determines when the cash inflow equals the initial investment. This method, which is described later in this chapter, does not adjust the value of cash flows occurring at different points in time. Instead, it favors the project that can return the initial investment first. While this method does not explicitly account for market interest rates, it does acknowledge the reduced value of a deferred payment.

There are two additional ways to evaluate projects that use the present value tools. The first is called net present value (NPV). As long as the present value of the cash return exceeds the investment, the project has an economic profit. The difference between the present value of cash flows received and the present value of cash flows invested is called the NPV of the project; it differs from profit as measured by accountants because it is profit above the return that the company should expect to earn from such a project. For the simple example involving only one immediate cash outflow and one deferred cash inflow, the formula is

$$\begin{aligned} NPV &= PV(\text{Cash Inflow}) - \text{Cash Outflow} \\ &= \frac{\text{Cash Inflow}}{(1 + \text{Rate})^t} - \text{Cash Outflow} \end{aligned} \quad (4.1)$$

Where t refers to the number of years between the cash outflow (investment) and the cash inflow.

Equation 4.1 is used to calculate the financial benefit of an investment. Equation 1.25 converts the value of the deferred cash inflow into a present value or a value that is equivalent to the deferred cash flow but occurring immediately. It is possible to compare the immediate cash investment to the present value of the cash returned. The difference between these two present value–adjusted cash flows is the net present value or NPV of the investment. If the investment is smaller than the present value of the cash returned, the investment is desirable. If the investment is larger than the present value of the cash return, the investment is undesirable. The company should not make the investment unless compelled by legal or regulatory requirements or other factors.

The present value Equation 1.25 in Chapter 1 can be arranged to calculate a rate of return called an Internal Rate of Return (IRR). Equation 4.2 assumes that the initial investment in the denominator is the present value as specified in Equation 1.25 and the cash inflow is the future value.

$$\text{Internal Rate of Return} = r_A = \sqrt[t]{\frac{\text{CashInflow}}{\text{CashOutflow}}} - 1 \quad (4.2)$$

Equation 4.2 will produce the annually compounded return (i.e., a percentage) that would make the present value equal to the future value. This is, of course, a different use for Equation 1.25. Previously, that equation was used to adjust the value of a single deferred cash flow. As adapted in Equation 4.2, we are now using two cash flows to measure an investment return.

Both the NPV and the IRR methodologies apply to business transactions involving more than one cash outflow (investment) and more than one inflow. This chapter develops the NPV and IRR tools as a method for making financial decisions.

CALCULATING NET PRESENT VALUE

It is easy to generalize the net present value formula. The sum of the inflow and outflow can be expanded to include multiple flows either into the company or out of it.

$$NPV = \frac{CF_1}{(1 + Rate)^1} + \frac{CF_2}{(1 + Rate)^2} \cdots + \frac{CF_N}{(1 + Rate)^N} \qquad (4.3)$$

In the more general formula that was presented, CF_1 usually represents the initial investment (an outflow and a negative cash flow). The rest of the cash flows are positive and represent the return on investment. In this case, the example would be very similar to the example described previously.

However, this formula can include other cash flow patterns. The invest-ment may be spread over several periods, or it may require costs to close manufacturing facilities when the product ends.

This more general formula for net present value uses the same present value mathematics as described throughout this book but incorporates (1) multiple cash flows and (2) netting of present value of the inflows and the present value of the outflows. This net present value formula provides a powerful tool to evaluate projects in the firm. Any project that can be de-scribed as a series of outflows (investments) and inflows (returns) can be evaluated as a net present value.

At the risk of oversimplifying a decision, the firm should invest in proj-ects that have a positive net present value. The firm should not only invest first in the projects that have the highest NPV, it should invest in *all* positive NPV projects, and it should reject *all* negative NPV projects. The firm should be willing to raise more capital to invest in all projects that have a return larger than that rate.

Determining the Discount Rate to Use

The NPV relies on a discounting rate to determine the present value of each cash flow. That rate is called the required return or hurdle rate. Companies usually use the Weighted Average Cost of Capital described in Chapter 3 as the required return used to calculate NPV.

NET PRESENT VALUE EXAMPLE

Table 4.1 presents a simple NPV calculation. For this example, a company can invest $1,000,000 and receive cash flows for the next five years as listed in the table. Table 4.1 discounts the cash flows at 14 percent.

The analysis of the project in Table 4.1 shows a net present value of –$84,061. In other words, the sum of the expected cash flows in Year 1 through Year 5 totals $1.3 million, but the present value of those cash flows equals only $915,939, or $84,061 less than the investment. Although the project should produce an accounting profit, the return is less than the 14 percent required return.

TABLE 4.1   Net Present Value of Cash Flows

Year	Cash Flow	Present Value
0	(1,000,000)	(1,000,000)
1	250,000	219,298
2	300,000	230,840
3	350,000	236,240
4	300,000	177,624
5	100,000	51,937
Net Present Value		(84,061)
Internal Rate of Return		10.22%

CALCULATING INTERNAL RATE OF RETURN

As suggested, there is another way to evaluate cash flows over multiple time horizons, although it also is derived from the fundamental PV and FV mathematics. The alternative method is called an internal rate of return and corresponds almost exactly to the rate of return calculation already presented in Equation 4.2.

For a clearer understanding of the internal rate of return calculation, consider the following additional information in Table 4.2 about the NPV of the project shown on Table 4.1.

Although the net present value of the project ranges from a low of ($273,152) at a 25 percent interest rate (and even more negatively, it would appear, at still higher rates) to a high of $300,000 at a zero interest rate, there is one interest rate (approximately 10.22 percent) at which the net present value is zero ($0). This rate is called the internal rate of return. A $1,000,000 investment in the new manufacturing strategy would earn an investment return of 10.22 percent.

TABLE 4.2   Net Present Value at Different
Required Returns

Rate	NPV
0.00%	300,000
5.00%	137,711
10.00%	5,163
10.22%	0
14.00%	(84,061)
20.00%	(195,923)
25.00%	(273,152)

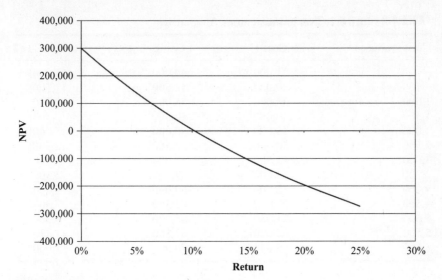

FIGURE 4.1 Net Present Value versus Return

To calculate the internal rate of return, the same present value adjustments are used to discount all payments back to the initial time period. The various discounted cash flows are summed (including positive and negative cash flows). This procedure is repeated for a number of interest rates in order to search for the rate at which the NPV equals zero.

Figure 4.1 displays the NPV of the project from Table 4.2. Figure 4.1 confirms that there is only one rate that would cause the NPV of this project to equal zero.

The internal rate of return can be viewed as a yield on the project. In the example given, the $1 million outflow can be viewed as an investment. The individual payments in Years 1 to 5 can be viewed as a return of principal and income.

It generally is not possible to solve for the internal rate of return algebraically. Instead, it is necessary to search for the rate. One simple way to find the IRR is to use the Excel function IRR.[*] Alternatively, it is easy to use SOLVER within Excel to search for the IRR for a series of cash flows. The questions at the end of the chapter and the answers at the back of the book demonstrate several ways to determine the IRR of a project.

Suppose a company could choose from two manufacturing strategies. Each method would include both fixed and variable costs, but the first method has a lower fixed cost and a higher variable cost than the second.

---

[*]The XIRR function can handle some cash flow patterns that IRR cannot analyze.

TABLE 4.3 Costs for Two Manufacturing Alternatives

Units Produced	Cost 1	Cost 2	Cost1 − Cost2
0	25,000	40,000	(15,000)
500	30,000	42,500	(12,500)
1,000	35,000	45,000	(10,000)
1,500	40,000	47,500	(7,500)
2,000	45,000	50,000	(5,000)
2,500	50,000	52,500	(2,500)
3,000	55,000	55,000	0
3,500	60,000	57,500	2,500
4,000	65,000	60,000	5,000
4,500	70,000	62,500	7,500
5,000	75,000	65,000	10,000
5,500	80,000	67,500	12,500
6,000	85,000	70,000	15,000

Table 4.3 lists a forecast of total costs for each alternative manufacturing strategy at different operating levels.

Assuming that the company produces 5,000 units, it can save $10,000 per year using the second method. As long as the company expects to produce more than 3,000 units per year, the second method results in a lower cost. Assume for now that the company can maintain a rate of 5,000 units indefinitely and that the cost savings would recur for 10 years. Under these circumstances, the company should immediately convert to the second process if there is no cost to convert.

However, if it costs $50,000 to convert from the process behind Cost 1 to the process behind Cost 2, the problem becomes a net present value problem. The company should spend the money if the present value of 10 years of savings exceeds the $50,000 investment.

CALCULATING YEARS TO PAYBACK

Some companies use a third method to evaluate projects; this is called the payback method. Refer back to the cash flows listed in Table 4.1. After making a $1 million initial investment, the company receives cash flows that eventually match and exceed the invested amount in the fourth year. In fact, the first four cash flows add up to $1.2 million, so the company receives a payback of the $1 million on or before the end of the fourth year. The time to payback is sometimes used to compare projects.

The payback method does not incorporate the present value methods described in Chapter 1. This method would not be able to consider the timing of the cash flows and would not provide a basis for comparing two projects with a similar payback period, even if one of the projects received substantial portions of the cash early and the second received much of the cash just before or on the payback date.

The payback method also ignores all the cash flows received after the payback date. Table 4.1 includes a cash flow of only $100,000 in the fifth year. Another project may have similar cash flows in the first four years but continue with large cash flows in Year 5 and beyond. The payback method would not consider the benefit of these additional cash flows.

Finally, the payback method assumes that receiving back cash inflow early is good and that a project with a shorter payback period is better than one with a longer payback period. This is appealing as a basis for comparing the risk of two or more projects. However, the risk of a project may have very little to do with the timing of the cash flows. In addition, the payback method does not account for the risks specific to a project.

FINANCIAL DECISION MAKING

Both NPV and IRR can be used to rank capital investments. If the cost of capital is known, a company should invest in all projects that have a positive NPV and never invest in a project with a negative NPV. If capital is scarce and additional capital cannot be raised, the projects with a positive NPV should be selected in a way to maximize the total NPV from the available investment funds.

Of course, this decision rule is much too simple for real-life applications. Companies should limit their focus to projects consistent with their corporate strategy. Also, for various reasons, corporations cannot accept all projects that appear attractive according to a financial decision-making model.

IRR can also be used to rank the profitability of individual projects. The company should invest in all projects whose IRR exceeds the company's cost of capital. Further, the company should not invest in projects that have a lower IRR than the company's required return.

There are several advantages to using NPV as a ranking tool instead of IRR. First, there can be more than one solution to the internal rate of return.* Second, ranking projects from highest to lowest IRR can sometimes

---

*Whenever there is a switch from negative to positive cash flows or from positive to negative cash flows, the possibility exists for an additional rate where the NPV equals zero.

lead to a different order than a ranking by NPV. If maximizing reported profits is a company objective, it should first invest in the projects with the highest NPV.

A company should invest in projects for which the sum of the present value of the cash outflows is less than the present value of the cash inflows. The NPV equals the sum of all projected cash flows. The present values of cash outflows are included as negative numbers, and the present values of cash inflows are included as positive numbers. It is shown later that this is another way of saying that the firm should invest in projects whose returns exceed the firm's cost of capital:

- Invest in A if Investment A < PV of cash returned from Investment A.
- Invest in A if the return r_A > of the firm's cost of capital.

For the simple examples involving two cash flows, this project return is easy to calculate. The foregoing return formula follows from some minor manipulations of the future value/present value equation.

THE ANNUITY FORMULA

The present value of a recurring payment is easy to calculate. A level payment is called an annuity. The present value of an annuity is easily priced from a standard formula. The value of an annual payment of $1 received at the end of each year is derived here. Using a cash flow of $1 is convenient, because all the cash flows in the numerator are equal. The value of any other cash flow will be the value of a $1 annuity times the cash flow.

$$PV = \frac{1}{1 + \text{Rate}} + \frac{1}{(1 + \text{Rate})^2} \cdots \frac{1}{(1 + \text{Rate})^N} \quad (4.4)$$

Multiply both sides of Equation 4.4 by $(1 + \text{Rate})$.

$$(1 + \text{Rate})PV = \frac{1 + \text{Rate}}{1 + \text{Rate}} + \frac{1 + \text{Rate}}{(1 + \text{Rate})^2} + \frac{1 + \text{Rate}}{(1 + \text{Rate})^3} \cdots \frac{1 + \text{Rate}}{(1 + \text{Rate})^N} \quad (4.5)$$

Simplify Equation 4.5 to remove the numerator terms.

$$(1 + \text{Rate})PV = 1 + \frac{1}{(1 + \text{Rate})^1} + \frac{1}{(1 + \text{Rate})^2} \cdots \frac{1}{(1 + \text{Rate})^{N-1}} \quad (4.6)$$

Subtract Equation 4.4 from Equation 4.6 and simplify. Most of the terms net to zero. Only the first term of Equation 4.6 and the last term of Equation 4.4 remain.

$$(1 + \text{Rate})\text{PV} - \text{PV} = 1 - \frac{1}{(1 + \text{Rate})^N} \qquad (4.7)$$

Factor out the variable PV from Equation 4.7.

$$(1 + \text{Rate} - 1)\text{PV} = 1 - \frac{1}{(1 + \text{Rate})^N} \qquad (4.8)$$

The left hand part of Equation 4.8 simplifies to Rate $*$ PV. Divide each side of Equation 4.8 by Rate to get Equation 4.9, which is the present value of a $1 annuity.

$$\text{PV} = \frac{1 - \dfrac{1}{(1 + \text{Rate})^N}}{\text{Rate}} \qquad (4.9)$$

For a discount rate of 8 percent and 10 payments, the present value is

$$\text{PV} = \frac{1 - \dfrac{1}{(1 + .08)^{10}}}{.08} = 6.710 \qquad (4.10)$$

For comparison, Table 4.4 sums the present value of 10 payments of $1 discounted at 8 percent. Table 4.4 validates the results of the formula in Equation 4.9.

This is the value of a $1 savings for 10 years, so a $10,000 savings would be worth $67,100.* If the savings required a $50,000 investment, the net present value of this project would be $67,100 $-50,000 = \$17,100$. It is worthwhile to make the investment of $50,000.

VALUING AN ANNUITY WITH MORE FREQUENT CASH FLOWS

The annuity formula in Equation 4.9 provides a quick and convenient way to value a series of annually occurring cash flows that are equal. The

---

*It is also possible to get the same result with the Excel function PV. In this case, the syntax would be "=PV(8%,10,10000)."

TABLE 4.4 Present Value of a $1 Annuity Discounted at 8 Percent

Year	Present Value	Sum	Excel Formula	Formula Result
1	0.926	0.926	$= (1 - (1/(1 + 8\%)^{\wedge}1))/8\%$	0.926
2	0.857	1.783	$= (1 - (1/(1 + 8\%)^{\wedge}2))/8\%$	1.783
3	0.794	2.577	$= (1 - (1/(1 + 8\%)^{\wedge}3))/8\%$	2.577
4	0.735	3.312	$= (1 - (1/(1 + 8\%)^{\wedge}4))/8\%$	3.312
5	0.681	3.993	$= (1 - (1/(1 + 8\%)^{\wedge}5))/8\%$	3.993
6	0.630	4.623	$= (1 - (1/(1 + 8\%)^{\wedge}6))/8\%$	4.623
7	0.583	5.206	$= (1 - (1/(1 + 8\%)^{\wedge}7))/8\%$	5.206
8	0.540	5.747	$= (1 - (1/(1 + 8\%)^{\wedge}8))/8\%$	5.747
9	0.500	6.247	$= (1 - (1/(1 + 8\%)^{\wedge}9))/8\%$	6.247
10	0.463	6.710	$= (1 - (1/(1 + 8\%)^{\wedge}10))/8\%$	6.710
25	0.146		$= (1 - (1/(1 + 8\%)^{\wedge}25))/8\%$	10.675
50	0.021		$= (1 - (1/(1 + 8\%)^{\wedge}50))/8\%$	12.233
100	0.000		$= (1 - (1/(1 + 8\%)^{\wedge}100))/8\%$	12.494

formula can be used to value semiannual, quarterly, or monthly cash flows as well. Suppose you need to value a bond that pays semiannual interest at an annual rate of 5 percent. The bond matures in exactly 5 years and will repay the principal of $100 at that time. Use a discount rate of 6 percent.

The bond pays a semiannual coupon of $100 ∗ 5%/2 or $2.50. This is an annuity of 10 payments. The annuity formula in 4.9 will price a semiannual annuity with the following adjustments:

$$PV = \frac{1 - \dfrac{1}{\left(1 + \dfrac{\text{Rate}}{2}\right)^{2*N}}}{\dfrac{\text{Rate}}{2}} \tag{4.11}$$

To adapt Equation 4.9, the semiannual rate is used instead of the annual rate. In other words, substitute the interest rate that pertains to a six-month period (half of the 6 percent annual rate) for the annual 6 percent rate. Also, use the number of semiannual periods (in this case, 10) instead of the number of years, as specified in Equation 4.9.

Pricing the 10 payments of $2.50 each, Equation 4.11 becomes

$$PV = 2.50 * \frac{1 - \dfrac{1}{\left(1 + \dfrac{6\%}{2}\right)^{10}}}{\dfrac{6\%}{2}} = 21.326 \tag{4.12}$$

USING THE PRESENT VALUE FORMULA AND THE ANNUITY FORMULA TO VALUE A BOND

The value of a bond includes the present value of the principal, repaid in five years or 10 semiannual payments. The present value uses Equation 1.25, modified for semiannual compounding.

$$PV = \frac{100}{\left(1 + \frac{6\%}{2}\right)^{2*5}} = 74.409 \tag{4.13}$$

The value of the bond equals the value of the coupon payments valued in the previous section plus the value of the principal payment: 21.326 + 74.409 = 95.735.

USING THE ANNUITY FORMULA TO VALUE A MORTGAGE

Equation 4.9 can also be used to value monthly mortgage payments. Suppose that a home buyer could afford to make a $1,500 per month mortgage payment. A bank will lend at 6 percent on a 30-year mortgage. The present value of 360 monthly payments equals the value of a loan that requires a $1,500 monthly payment.

$$PV = 1,500 * \frac{1 - \frac{1}{\left(1 + \frac{6\%}{12}\right)^{360}}}{\frac{6\%}{12}} = 250,187 \tag{4.14}$$

To adapt the annuity formula for monthly payments, the number of years is changed to the number of months (360 in Equation 4.14). Also, the monthly interest rate (6 percent divided by 12 months) is used in Equation 4.14 instead of the annual 6 percent rate used in Equation 4.9.

NPV USING THE ANNUITY FORMULA

Suppose a company is considering an investment that would require cash outflows of $500,000 at the end of one year and continuing for two more years. Following the completion of the investment, the company expects to

TABLE 4.5 NPV Using the Annuity Formula

Year	Cash Flow	Present Value	
1	($500,000)	($434,783)	
2	(500,000)	(378,072)	
3	(500,000)	(328,758)	($1,141,613)
4	350,000	200,114	
5	350,000	174,012	
6	350,000	151,315	
7	350,000	131,578	
8	350,000	114,416	
9	350,000	99,492	
10	350,000	86,515	
11	350,000	75,230	
12	350,000	65,418	
13	350,000	56,885	$1,154,973
	NPV	13,360	

receive $350,000 one year later, continuing for a total of 10 years. These cash flows are listed in Table 4.5. Discount all cash flows at 15 percent (annual compounding).

The NPV of the cash flows can also be valued as a 3-year annuity valued with Equation 4.9 using the investment cash outflows of $500,000 each plus a 10-year annuity deferred for three additional years that has payments (cash inflows) of $350,00 per year. The annuity formula in Equation 4.9 discounts the 10 payments of $350,000 to the end of year 3. This second annuity term is discounted for 3 additional years. Equation 4.15 adapts Equation 4.9 to handle the valuation.

$$PV = -500,000 \left(\frac{1 - \dfrac{1}{(1 + 15\%)^3}}{15\%} \right) + \frac{350,000}{(1 + 15\%)^3} \left(\frac{1 - \dfrac{1}{(1 + 15\%)^{10}}}{15\%} \right)$$

(4.15)

The first term equals –$1,141,613, which exactly matches the present value of the three cash outflows subtotaled in Table 4.5. The second term equals $1,154,973, which matches the subtotal of the 10 cash inflows subtotaled in Table 4.5.

VALUING A PERPETUITY

Table 4.4 documents that each additional year that an annuity exists adds less to the value of the annuity. A 2-year annuity is worth $.86 more than a 1-year annuity (i.e., the present value of the second cash flow), while a 10-year annuity is worth $.46 more than a 9-year annuity. By 100 years, the incremental cash flow is worth almost zero. As a result, the present values of very long annuities approach a finite value, as confirmed visually in Figure 4.2.

An annuity that lasts forever is called a perpetuity. It is possible to develop a formula for the value of a perpetuity. In this case, the formula is actually simpler than the annuity formula in Equation 4.9. To show this, the derivation of the value of an annuity is extended to infinity.

$$PV = \frac{1}{1+\text{Rate}} + \frac{1}{(1+\text{Rate})^2} \cdots \frac{1}{(1+\text{Rate})^\infty} \qquad (4.16)$$

Applying the same technique used in Equation 4.5, we multiply both sides of Equation 4.16 by $(1 + \text{Rate})$.

$$(1+\text{Rate})PV = \frac{1+\text{Rate}}{1+\text{Rate}} + \frac{1+\text{Rate}}{(1+\text{Rate})^2} + \frac{1+\text{Rate}}{(1+\text{Rate})^3} \cdots \frac{1+\text{Rate}}{(1+\text{Rate})^\infty} \qquad (4.17)$$

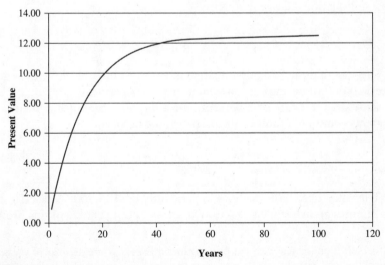

FIGURE 4.2 Present Value of $1 Annuity

Then simplify Equation 4.17 to remove the numerator terms.

$$(1 + \text{Rate})\text{PV} = 1 + \frac{1}{(1 + \text{Rate})^1} + \frac{1}{(1 + \text{Rate})^2} \cdots \frac{1}{(1 + \text{Rate})^{\infty-1}} \quad (4.18)$$

Subtract Equation 4.16 from Equation 4.18 and simplify. Most of the terms net to zero. Only the first term of Equation 4.18 and the last term of Equation 4.16 remain.

$$(1 + \text{Rate})\text{PV} - \text{PV} = 1 - \frac{1}{(1 + \text{Rate})^{\infty}} \quad (4.19)$$

Factor out the PV variable from Equation 4.19.

$$(1 + \text{Rate} - 1)\text{PV} = 1 - \frac{1}{(1 + \text{Rate})^{\infty}} \quad (4.20)$$

The left-hand part of Equation 4.20 simplifies to Rate $*$ PV. Divide each side of Equation 4.20 by Rate to get Equation 4.21, which is the present value of a \$1 annuity that continues forever.

$$\text{PV} = \frac{1 - \dfrac{1}{(1 + \text{Rate})^{\infty}}}{\text{Rate}} \quad (4.21)$$

The second term in the numerator equals zero for all positive interest rates, so Equation 4.21 simplifies to:

$$\text{PV} = \frac{1}{\text{Rate}} \quad (4.22)$$

Suppose that the \$50,000 investment presented in Table 4.3 would generate \$10,000 of savings in manufacturing costs per year indefinitely. Use the same discount rate of 8 percent. For a discount rate of 8 percent and payments continuing forever, the present value of \$1 is

$$\text{PV} = \frac{1}{.08} = 12.50 \quad (4.23)$$

The value of \$10,000 savings in perpetuity is \$125,000.* Since the savings requires an investment of \$50,000, the net present value of this project

---

* This result is consistent with the PV function in Excel. As the number of years increases, the present value stops increasing because the long-delayed cash payments are worthless in present value terms.

TABLE 4.6 Present Value of a $1 Annuity at Various Rates

Rate	Excel Formula	Formula Result
1%	=1/1%	100.000
5%	=1/5%	20.000
10%	=1/10%	10.000
15%	=1/15%	6.667
20%	=1/20%	5.000

would be $125,000 − 50,000 = $75,000. Therefore, it is worthwhile to make the investment of $50,000. Table 4.6 applies Equation 4.22 at various discount rates to value a $1 perpetual annuity or perpetuity.

VALUING A GROWTH PERPETUITY

For good measure, it is possible that the level of predicted cash flows could grow from period to period. Suppose that the first payment (or cost savings in the example from Table 4.3) occurs at the end of Year 1. The savings grow at a rate of Growth and are discounted at a rate, represented as Rate.

$$
PV = \frac{1}{1+\text{Rate}} + \frac{1+\text{Growth}}{(1+\text{Rate})^2} + \frac{(1+\text{Growth})^2}{(1+\text{Rate})^3}
$$
$$
+ \frac{(1+\text{Growth})^3}{(1+\text{Rate})^4} \cdots \frac{(1+\text{Growth})^{\infty-1}}{(1+\text{Rate})^\infty} \qquad (4.24)
$$

Following the procedure used here, multiply both sides by a term so that when the two equations are subtracted, most of the terms disappear:

$$
\frac{(1+\text{Rate})}{(1+\text{Growth})} PV = \frac{1}{(1+\text{Growth})^1} + \frac{1}{(1+\text{Rate})}
$$
$$
+ \frac{(1+\text{Growth})^1}{(1+\text{Rate})^2} + \cdots \frac{(1+\text{Growth})^{\infty-2}}{(1+\text{Rate})^{\infty-1}} \qquad (4.25)
$$

The subtraction is also similar to the preceding manipulation.

$$
\frac{(1+\text{Rate})}{(1+\text{Growth})} PV - PV = \frac{1}{1+\text{Growth}} - \frac{(1+\text{Growth})^{\infty-1}}{(1+\text{Rate})^\infty} \qquad (4.26)
$$

Factor out the variable PV.

$$\left[\frac{(1 + \text{Rate})}{(1 + \text{Growth})} - 1\right]\text{PV} = \frac{1}{1 + \text{Growth}} - \frac{(1 + \text{Growth})^{\infty - 1}}{(1 + \text{Rate})^{\infty}} \qquad (4.27)$$

Combine the terms in the square bracket.

$$\left[\frac{1 + \text{Rate} - 1 - \text{Growth}}{(1 + \text{Growth})}\right]\text{PV} = -\frac{(1 + \text{Growth})^{\infty - 1}}{(1 + \text{Rate})^{\infty}} \qquad (4.28)$$

Move the denominator from the left side to the right and simplify.

$$(\text{Rate} - \text{Growth})\text{PV} = 1 - \frac{(1 + \text{Growth})^{\infty}}{(1 + \text{Rate})^{\infty}} \qquad (4.29)$$

The second term on the right-hand size equals zero for all Rate > Growth. Therefore,

$$\text{PV} = \frac{1}{\text{Rate} - \text{Growth}} \qquad (4.30)$$

for Rate > Growth and PV = infinite (or perhaps undefined) for all other cases.

Extending the problem from Table 4.3, if the initial savings is $10,000, the discount rate is 8 percent, and the growth in savings is 3 percent, the present value of $1 in savings is

$$\text{PV} = \frac{1}{.08 - .03} = 20.00 \qquad (4.31)$$

The savings of $20 * $10,000 or $200,000 well exceeds the investment of $50,000.

INTRODUCTION TO UNCERTAINTY

There remains one problem with the analysis of this $50,000 investment. The NPV calculations assumed away the possibility of other levels of sales and production. More realistically, the level is uncertain. If production is below 3,000 units, no investment is justified because the original process is cheaper than the second process. In a real-world situation, that uncertainty must be part of the decision process. Chapter 5 develops ways to handle uncertainty.

TABLE 4.7 NPV for Two Manufacturing Alternatives

Units Produced	Cost 1	Cost 2	Cost1 – Cost2	NPV
0	25,000	40,000	(15,000)	(237,500)
500	30,000	42,500	(12,500)	(206,250)
1,000	35,000	45,000	(10,000)	(175,000)
1,500	40,000	47,500	(7,500)	(143,750)
2,000	45,000	50,000	(5,000)	(112,500)
2,500	50,000	52,500	(2,500)	(81,250)
3,000	55,000	55,000	0	(50,000)
3,500	60,000	57,500	2,500	(18,750)
4,000	65,000	60,000	5,000	12,500
4,500	70,000	62,500	7,500	43,750
5,000	75,000	65,000	10,000	75,000
5,500	80,000	67,500	12,500	106,250
6,000	85,000	70,000	15,000	137,500

The variable cost analysis from Table 4.3 is reproduced here as Table 4.7 with the net present value for each level of activity. The NPV discounts perpetual savings from each operating level at 8 percent and with no growth in savings (net of the $50,000 investment).

Assume, in addition, that there is a 10 percent probability of operating at 3,500 units, a 20 percent probability of operating at 4,000 units, a 30 percent probability of operating at 4,500 units, a 30 percent probability of operating at 5,000 units, and a 10 percent probability of operating at 5,500 units.* Under these assumptions, the expected value of the present value of the cost savings is

$$\text{NPV}_{\text{Expected}} = 10\% * (18,750) + 20\% * 12,500 + 30\% * 43,750 \\ + 30\% * 75,000 + 10\% * 106,250 = 46,875 \quad (4.32)$$

Under these assumptions, it would still be attractive to invest the $50,000 for an uncertain savings of $2,500 to $10,000 per year, because the NPV values include the cost of the investment. The NPV values in Table 4.7 exceed the cost of the $50,000 investment by $46,875 for the scenarios and probabilities assumed in Equation 4.32.

---

*The other levels are assumed to be unlikely and are given a probability of zero (0). This overly simplifies the uncertainty, of course, because the units change over time. Also, it is likely that some of the probability should be allocated to levels of output between these 500-unit divisions. More elaborate methods of handling the uncertainty are beyond the scope of this chapter.

Some questions posed by the analysis in Table 4.7 remain unanswered. Is it possible to operate at levels other than the levels listed in the table? How are the probabilities for each operating level determined? Is 8 percent the right level to use to discount the predicted savings in light of the uncertainty present in the investment? Chapter 5 introduces a number of tools to value uncertain cash flows.

CONCLUSION

The present value method introduced in Chapter 1 has now been expanded into a model for making financial decisions. The formula for present value taken from Chapter 1 provides the basis for calculating the net present value of a project. The same tools are used to calculate the internal rate of return on a project. These tools provide a method for evaluating a project or comparing two or more projects.

4.1. Suppose your current income would permit you to make a $2,000 per month mortgage payment. What is the maximum loan you can get if mortgage rates are 5 percent for a 15-year loan? What loan amount could you borrow at 5.5 percent on a 30-year loan?

4.2. Camilla needs to borrow $400,000. Mortgage rates are at 6 percent for both a 15-year and a 30-year loan. How much could she reduce her monthly cash payment by picking the loan with the lower payment?

Use the following assumptions for the two projects under review.

Cash Flows of Two Projects

Year	Project 1 Cash Flow	Project 2 Cash Flow
0	($10,000,000)	($10,000,000)
1	3,000,000	1,700,000
2	3,000,000	1,700,000
3	3,000,000	1,700,000
4	3,000,000	1,700,000
5	0	1,700,000
6	0	1,700,000
7	0	1,700,000
8	0	1,700,000
9	0	1,700,000
10	0	1,700,000

4.3a. Calculate the payback period for each of these two projects.

4.3b. Based solely on the payback period, which investment appears to be more attractive?

4.4a. Assume that the cost of capital for the company considering the projects previously mentioned is 14 percent compounded annually. What is the net present value of each project whose cash flows are listed in Table Q.2?

4.4b. Based solely on the net present value of Project 1 and Project 2, which investment appears to be more attractive?

4.5. Your company issued debt two years ago with an 8 percent semiannual coupon. The issue now has five years remaining until maturity. The fair market price of the debt is 104.25 (per $100 face amount). What is the pretax cost of debt for the company?

4.6. Suppose the 8 percent bond described in Question 4.5 matured in exactly 4.75 years. The market price is still 104.25. What is the company's pretax cost of debt capital?

CHAPTER 5

Techniques for Handling Uncertainty

INTRODUCTION

The previous chapters provided a basis for valuing an investment with cash flows that occur at different points in time. The present value analysis adjusts the nominal cash flows to compensate for both the time value of money and risk. A risk-free rate, often defined as a U.S. Treasury or Libor yield, adjusts for time. By using a higher rate, the method is extended to cash flows from projects that have risk.

The risks are numerous and may be impossible to predict. The size of the cash flows may be larger or smaller than the cash flows predicted. The timing of the cash flows may be uncertain, arriving either earlier or later than expected. Many forecasted cash inflows may never arrive, and unforecasted cash outflows may reduce the profitability of an investment.

This chapter introduces techniques for including knowledge about the uncertainty of forecasted cash flows. Like Chapter 2, this chapter is primarily about statistical methods for including probabilities in the analysis of uncertain outcomes. Chapter 6 uses these techniques to value uncertain cash flows.

USING SCENARIO ANALYSIS

Businesses frequently make multiple forecasts. In some cases, the forecasts include a most likely forecast along with a pessimistic and an optimistic forecast. Frequently these scenarios reflect specific reasons why each scenario might occur. Sometimes, the scenarios reflect the impact of several uncertain factors that interact to create the pessimistic and optimistic scenarios. Frequently, managers may be able to estimate the chance of some of the scenarios. Other times, the managers can produce only gut-feel probabilities that may not reflect all the information the manager has about market conditions.

This chapter will present two methods for handling scenarios. The first method relies on potential outcomes to determine theoretical probabilities. We will use trees to organize the scenarios to make clear how they interact. The second method is called Monte Carlo simulation. Monte Carlo simulation relies on particular facts to build an experiment, which is then used to sample possible outcomes. This method produces a large number of scenarios called paths. Because of the large number of scenarios, little attention is focused on particular outcomes. Instead, the many outcomes provide information about the average or expected outcome and about the amount of uncertainty in the outcome.

Introduction to Trees

Trees can be used to arrange and organize uncertain outcomes. For example, suppose you had a new technology that you hoped to protect by patent. (See Figure 5.1.) There is a 60 percent chance that you will be granted a patent. If the patent is awarded, there is a 70 percent chance that you will be successful in defending the patent from infringement. If the patent is not granted, there is a 45 percent chance that you will be able to protect trade secrets and trademarks to establish a strong market position.

The three uncertainties create four scenarios. If the patent is awarded and the company successfully defends the patent (Scenario 1), the company

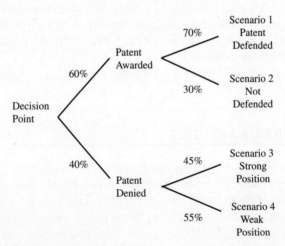

FIGURE 5.1   Patent Protection Tree

is in the most favorable scenario. There is a 60 percent chance of obtaining a patent award and a 70 percent probability of defending the patent. The chance of that scenario is thus 60 percent * 70 percent or 42 percent.

The least favorable scenario occurs when the company does not obtain the patent and is not able to use trade secrets and trademarks to improve its competitive position. This is Scenario 4. The chance of experiencing this scenario is 40 percent * 55 percent or 22 percent.

Scenario 2 assumes that the company is awarded a patent but is not successful in using that patent to prevent competition. The chance of experiencing this scenario is 60 percent * 30 percent or 18 percent.

Scenario 3 assumes that the company fails to receive a patent but is able to rely on trade secrets and trademarks to secure some market protection. The chance of experiencing this scenario is 40 percent * 45 percent or 18 percent.

The sum of these four probabilities is 42 percent + 22 percent + 18 percent + 18 percent, which is 100 percent. This predictable result provides a cross check that the scenarios constitute all possible outcomes. If the probabilities sum to less than 100 percent, the tree does not reflect all possibilities (i.e., the tree needs additional branches) or the probabilities for each uncertain event are unrealistic. If the probabilities sum to greater than 100 percent, the tree probabilities are also incorrect.

The probabilities created this way can be used to determine the expected or average cash flows. No details about the cash flows are provided in each of the four scenarios. The company must still forecast the cash flows under each scenario. However, the company has a way to combine expectations from separate events and create a method for determining the probability of each of the outcomes.

Probabilities such as the preceding example provide a basis for valuing uncertain cash flows. The method, however, only averages the scenarios. It does not remove the uncertainty and it does not account for the investors' attitude about risk. For example, it might be the case that profitability varies tremendously in each of the four scenarios. The profitability of other projects may be less sensitive to the assumptions in the four scenarios. Investors and companies seeking to avoid risk prefer to undertake the project that produces consistent results across various scenarios.

USING MONTE CARLO SIMULATION

Monte Carlo simulation consists of a set of techniques employed to conduct experiments using computers to better understand randomness in real-world situations. The simulations are not real, but they can reveal accurate information if properly constructed and properly configured. The technique relies on random number generators (see the following discussion) that can create a sequence of realistic hypothetical outcomes.

Random Number Generators

Computer-based random number generators were created soon after computers were invented. The development of improved number generators paralleled the development and availability of computers. Random number generators have long been used by bookmaking, sports betting, and other gambling enterprises. Most casino games rely on cards, roulette wheels, or dice to create random outcomes. The "numbers game" or "numbers racket" refers to a private lottery driven by real-world random numbers, such as the lower digits of the closing level of the Dow Jones Industrial Average or a formula fed by data from a horse track. Similarly, sports outcomes determine the payoffs of countless bets both among private individuals and with professionals. Modern government-sponsored lotteries usually rely on a physical action (such as pulling balls from an urn) to determine the winners.

These real-world random number generators have their equivalent in Monte Carlo simulations. Computer modelers who demand truly random numbers can access a variety of sources. These hardware devices use the random (or very nearly random) nature of atomic particles, heat, or some other physical phenomenon, often built into a convenient device that plugs into the back of a computer.

Here, the focus is on random number generators developed by computer scientists. These numbers are more accurately called pseudo-random numbers, because they closely resemble random numbers and may act much like truly random numbers. They are, however, determined by the choice of algorithm and generally can be exactly reproduced over and over again in the same sequence. In this chapter, pseudo-random numbers are referred to as random numbers, with no distinction being made between true random numbers, hardware-generated random numbers, and pseudo-random numbers.

One example of a pseudo-random number is a linear congruential generator. There are many types of such generators, and the example that follows is both primitive and unreliable. Nevertheless, it serves to explain how random number generators operate, to demonstrate some advantages of these numbers for simulation, and to highlight some concerns.

Start with an arbitrary value, chosen by the user. In this example, choose 5. Then multiply this number by 13, and then add 17. Divide the result by 15 to the nearest integer then calculate the remainder. This remainder, 7, is the first random number. Then, repeat this process, starting with 7 and applying the same formula. The formula produces a remainder of 3. Equation 5.1 summarizes the formula.

$$V_{t+1} = (A * V_t + B)\,\mathrm{mod}\,M \qquad (5.1)$$

where V_t = successive random numbers, $A = 13$, $B = 17$, $M = 15$, and $V_0 = 5$.

The modulo function (or mod) is equal to the remainder after M is divided into the value in parentheses. The results of successive values appear in Table 5.1.

The first column is the "trial" or a count of the number of random numbers generated. The second column is the remainder created by Equation 5.1 at each step. The starting value or "seed" is the value listed as Trial 0. Notice that, after 12 numbers, the value 5 comes up again. From this point the pattern will repeat exactly as shown in the table.

The third column is a transformation of the number in the middle column. The remainder can take on any value between 0 and 14 (although the values 4, 9, and 14 don't happen to appear in this series before the pattern repeats). By dividing the middle column by 14 (more generally, divide by $M - 1$), the numbers in the third column must range between 0 and 1.

For example, the starting number is 5. $V_1 = (13 * 5 + 17)\,\mathrm{mod}\,15$. The value in parentheses is 82; 15 divides into 82 with a remainder of 7, which is the first random number generated in Table 5.1. This value can be

TABLE 5.1   Random Numbers Produced by Equation 5.1

Trial	Value	Value Transformed
0	5	n.a.
1	7	0.5000
2	3	0.2143
3	11	0.7857
4	10	0.7143
5	12	0.8571
6	8	0.5714
7	1	0.0714
8	0	0.0000
9	2	0.1429
10	13	0.9286
11	6	0.4286
12	5	0.3571

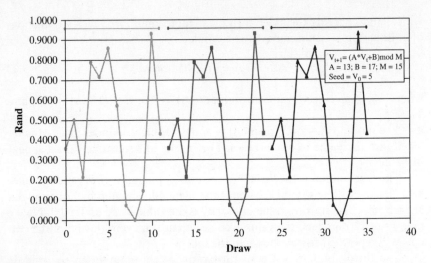

FIGURE 5.2 Simple Random Number Generator

transformed into a number between 0 and 1 by dividing V_1 or 7 by $M - 1$ or 14. As a result, the first random number is 0.5000.

The value 7 is used to generate the next number. $V_2 = (13 * 7 + 17)$ mod 15 or 108 mod 15. The next remainder is 3. This number divided by 14 is .2143.

Figure 5.2 shows a graph of the successive values produced by Equation 5.1.

Within a block, the numbers appear to be random. However, the number sequence repeats and will continue to repeat over and over again. Whenever you start with 5, Equation 5.1 will generate exactly this sequence of numbers. Whenever 5 recurs in the series, the pattern will repeat. While there is an obvious advantage in being able to conduct different experiments using the same sequence of trials, the pattern obvious in the trials makes this generator unusable.

Fortunately, other values for A, B, and M can produce much better trials, with millions of numbers occurring before they repeat; thus, producing numbers that closely resemble truly random numbers. There are other types of generators as well. Finally, additional randomness can be introduced by combining random generators. For example, one algorithm generates a collection of random numbers in advance. When a random number is needed, it is randomly drawn from the collection. A new random number is created and placed into the collection of available random numbers for future use.

UNIFORM RANDOM NUMBERS

The most widely available random number generators produce uniformly distributed random numbers. A plot of random numbers is shown in Figure 5.3.

The random numbers from the Excel function RAND() are plotted successively. The values range from 0 up to (but excluding) 1 and do not cluster around any level. Although there are some gaps and clusters, they also result from randomness. The values from RAND() appear in different locations each time these 250 trials are repeated.

TRANSFORMING UNIFORM DISTRIBUTIONS

The samples in Figure 5.3 can be used as random numbers without further transformation. However, researchers frequently need other types of random numbers than can easily be created from the values in Figure 5.3. For example, a coin toss has only two outcomes. It is simple to classify all values equal to .50 and below as heads and all other values as tails. To convert these uniform numbers into a coin toss (e.g., 1 for heads and 0 for tails), an IF statement can be used to assign either 0 or 1 to the trial. Alternatively, these values can be converted to 1 or 0 by simply rounding up or down to the nearest integer. Excel and many programming languages have a function to round. Excel has a function called ROUND (input, number of digits). To use this function, round the random number to zero digits. This function rounds all values from .50 and above up to 1 and values between 0 and .50 down to 0. Excel's ROUND function rounds .50 up to 1.

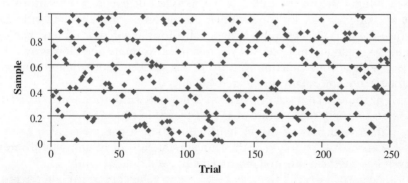

FIGURE 5.3 Uniform Distribution

To convert a uniformly distributed random number (ranging between 0 and 1) into draws from a deck of cards, a series of IF statements could be used:

IF $(X < 0.019230769)$ (i.e., 1/52, it is an ace of clubs)

ELSE IF $(X < 0.038461538)$ (i.e., 2/52, it is a two of clubs)

ELSE IF $(X < 0.057692308)$ (i.e., 3/52, it is a three of clubs)

And so on.

Specific computer languages implement this syntax slightly differently.

Simulating a draw from 52 cards may be simpler if the uniform random number is converted into a number between 1 and 52. For example, multiply the random number by 52, add 1, then truncate to an integer (i.e., ignore the values to the right of the decimal point). The result ranges from 1 to 52. Each of the values is equally likely to occur.

The values 1 to 52 might be used directly in an experiment, or they might be converted to some other form. Computer programmers can use this value to point to a value in a table or array. The logical structure called the CASE statement can be used to control a program based on the 52 possible values. These applications are beyond the scope of this chapter.

Converting a Uniformly Distributed Random Variable into a Normally Distributed Random Variable

Monte Carlo simulation frequently requires normally distributed random variables. The normal distribution is a probability distribution. In routine use, an input (frequently called "z") is used to calculate a particular probability. For example, software routines in computer languages and in Excel return the probability of observing a value for the outcome (z) less than or equal to the input. In Excel, see the functions Norminv and Normsinv. Use the inverse normal function to transform a uniformly distributed random variable into a normally distributed value.

The standard normal distribution (a normal distribution with a mean of zero and a standard deviation of 1) is displayed in Figure 5.4.

Other distributions can be built with different parameters. For example, a normal distribution with a higher standard deviation would stack fewer balls in the center and more to the left and right of center.

The normal distribution can take on any value, but to explain the process of inverting, picture the distribution as a pile of marbles. Approximately two-thirds of the marbles are piled between +1 and −1. Nineteen

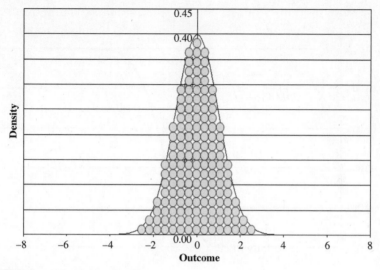

FIGURE 5.4   Normal Distribution

out of every twenty marbles are within +2 and −2. Finally, although these marbles appear to be stacked directly on top of each other as in a histogram, they should be thought of as slightly off-center from each other.

A draw from a uniform distribution picks a particular marble that represents a particular probability (labeled "density" here). Reading off the location on the Density or Y axis yields a random variable that acts like a normally distributed random variable because most of the marbles are near the mean.

Figure 5.5 presents the same information in a slightly different form. In Figure 5.5, the probability of being at or to the left of (less than) a particular point is graphed on the Y axis, now labeled Probability.

At the left, at −4, for example, 0 marbles appear under the curve. At the mean (the vertical line at zero in both Figures 5.4 and 5.5), half of the marbles are located to the left. At the point +4, all (or 100 percent) of the marbles appear to the left. This probability or density ranges from 0 to 1 or 0 percent to 100 percent. Each probability corresponds to picking a marble, so the chance of picking a value near the mean is high, and the chance of picking a marble at an extreme point in the tail of the curve is small.

This process of finding an X value given a Y value is called inverting. In this case, we are inverting the cumulative probability under the normal distribution. The uniformly distributed random variable is inverted in Excel

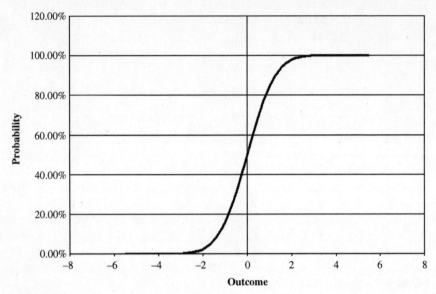

FIGURE 5.5 Cumulative Normal Distribution

using the NORMINV function. Similar functions can be found in many programming languages using different syntaxes. The format in Excel is

$$= \text{NORMINV(Prob, Mean, Standard Deviation)} \qquad (5.2)$$

where: Prob = a random, uniformly distributed variable
Mean = desired mean for the sample of random numbers
Standard Deviation = desired standard deviation for the sample of random numbers

For example, we know that half of normally distributed points are less than the mean and half are above. The Excel function NORMINV(.5, 0, 1) returns 0, where the first input is the probability, the second is the mean and the third is the standard deviation. The Excel function NORMSINV(.5) for a standard normal distribution (a normal distribution with mean of 0 and a standard deviation of 1) also returns 0, where the input is the probability.

The preceding method is called inverse transform sampling. It is intuitive and reliable, but other methods are also available, such as the Box-Muller transformation. If execution speed is important, the Box-Muller transformation will probably be faster than the method described here, but there is no preinstalled Box-Muller function available in Excel.

Creating Two Correlated Normally Distributed Random Variables

Monte Carlo simulation can be helpful in understanding the impact of two or more variables that are uncertain. To complicate matters, these variables may tend (weakly or strongly) to move together. Although it takes several steps, it is not difficult to create two normally distributed random numbers that are correlated. The example that follows demonstrates the steps. Suppose that you wanted to create one series of random numbers with a mean of 300,000 and a standard deviation of 250,000 and a second series of random numbers with a mean of 500,000 and a standard deviation of 500,000. Finally, assume that the correlation between these two series should be .40.

The first step is to generate two series of uniformly distributed numbers. Table 5.2 shows part of a table of 2,000 draws (1,000 for each series, labeled U_1 and U_2).

These two series will be uncorrelated (i.e., they have a correlation equal to or close to zero).

The next step is to convert these numbers to standard normal random numbers. A standard normal series has a mean of zero and a standard deviation of 1. The Excel function NORMINV converts these uniform numbers to normal. Table 5.3 shows part of a table of 2,000 normally distributed random numbers (1,000 for each series labeled N_1 and N_2).

The sample used to complete Table 5.3 has means of 0.011 and 0.010, as listed at the bottom of each series. The standard deviation of these random numbers is 0.985 and 1.004. The correlation between the series is 0.019. As expected, each series has a sample mean near the mean of 0 and a sample standard deviation near 1, and the two series are nearly uncorrelated.

TABLE 5.2 Uniform Random Numbers

Draw	U_1	U_2
1	0.671	0.935
2	0.436	0.647
3	0.967	0.023
.	.	.
.	.	.
.	.	.
1,000	0.660	0.232
Mean	0.503	0.504
Standard Deviation	0.287	0.291

TABLE 5.3   Standard Normal Random Numbers

Draw	N_1	N_2
1	0.442	1.514
2	−0.161	0.377
3	1.837	−1.993
.	.	.
.	.	.
1,000	0.411	−0.731
Mean	0.011	0.010
Standard Deviation	0.985	1.004
Correlation	0.019	

The next step is to create the desired correlation between the two normal series and adjust the series to match the desired mean and standard deviation for each series. The first series averages approximately 0, so multiplying each value by the desired standard deviation would expand the range of values but not shift the mean. In Table 5.4, all of the standard normal numbers labeled N_1 now also include the 300,000 added to match the desired mean. The series averages approximately 300,000 and has a standard deviation approximately matching the desired standard deviation. The adjustment appears in Equation 5.3.

$$X_1 = \text{Mean}_1 + \text{SD}_1 * N_1 \qquad (5.3)$$

for each number in the X_1 series. To create X_1 in Table 5.4, 300,000 was used as Mean_1 and 250,000 was used as SD_1.

TABLE 5.4   Correlated Normal Random Numbers

Draw	X_1	X_2	$X_1 + X_2$
1	410,406	1,281,986	1,692,391
2	259,766	640,355	900,121
3	759,151	−46,172	712,979
.	.	.	.
.	.	.	.
1,000	402,824	247,230	650,054
Mean	302,625	507,262	809,887
Standard Deviation	246,241	503,916	644,827
Correlation	0.408		

The second series in Table 5.4 labeled X_2 is created from both N_1 and N_2. The combination creates the desired correlation. The formula for determining each X_2 is presented in Equation 5.4.

$$X_2 = \text{Mean}_2 + \text{SD}_2 * \left(N_1 * \text{Corr} + N_2 * \sqrt{1 - \text{Corr}^2} \right) \qquad (5.4)$$

for each number in the X_2 series. To create X_2 in Table 5.4, 500,000 was used as Mean_2, 500,000 was used as SD_2, and .40 was used as Corr. The results of the transformations appear in Table 5.4.

The example in Table 5.4 also demonstrates the diversification effect in a portfolio, as discussed in Chapter 2. The mean of the sum of X_1 and X_2 is 809,887, close to the predicted value of 800,000 (300,000 + 500,000). The standard deviation of the sum of X_1 and X_2 is 644,827, close to the predicted value of 642,262 (square root (250,000 ^ 2 + 500,000 ^ 2 + 2 * .4 * 250,000 * 500,000)). The standard deviation of the sum is below the sum of the standard deviations (250,000 + 750,000 = 750,000).

The same procedure could be used to test the impact of two uncertainties on a business investment. For example, suppose that a proposed new product could produce an expected unit sales volume (the mean of possible sales scenarios) but is also subject to uncertain raw materials costs. If the sales volume is unrelated to the raw materials costs, correlated random values are not necessary. However, if these materials costs impact unit sales (one example would be the price of oil and the demand for oil-drilling services), correlated samples are necessary to understand the uncertainty of a project.

Creating More Than Two Correlated Normally Distributed Random Variables

The procedure presented in the previous section demonstrated how to create two series of correlated random numbers. A related procedure can produce a series of three or more correlated random variables. The general procedure is the same. First, generate three or more standard normal (independent) series as in Table 5.3. Then blend together the returns to create the desired correlation between each series.

The mathematics could get messy, but fortunately the problem can be stated as one involving matrix mathematics. This technique is beyond the scope of this chapter. Readers who want to learn about this technique should read about how a mathematical operation called the Cholesky Decomposition can be used to create weights and how matrix multiplication can be used to blend together the returns from several normal random samples.

Converting a Uniformly Distributed Random Variable into a Lognormally Distributed Random Variable

Many times, it is necessary to understand the impact of price changes on a business investment. Prices may include sales prices, which directly affect revenue. The price of raw materials may also be uncertain, which can affect the cost of goods sold.

Prices generally cannot be negative, but the normal distribution can create situations in which negative prices are included in an analysis. One alternative is to use the lognormal distribution, in part because negative prices cannot occur with the lognormal distribution. The lognormal distribution also matches the price behavior of many assets better than the normal distribution.

The lognormal distribution is probably the most commonly used distribution in finance, especially for securities pricing. If returns (compounded continuously) are normally distributed (i.e., they resemble Figure 5.4 modified to match a particular mean and standard deviation for return), the price of the security is lognormally distributed. Recall that

$$P_{t+1} = P_t * e^{\text{Rate}*\text{Time}} \tag{5.5}$$

and

$$\ln \frac{P_{t+1}}{P_t} = \text{Rate} * \text{Time} \tag{5.6}$$

Equation 5.7 applies Equation 5.5 to find a centering point.

$$\text{Adjusted Forward Price} = Spot * e^{(\text{Rate}-\text{Dividend})*\text{Time}-\frac{\sigma^2}{2*\text{Time}}} \tag{5.7}$$

The adjusted forward price or centering price in Equation 5.7 will result in an average price equal to the forward price. The forward price is closely related to the future value calculated in Chapter 1. The spot or current price for immediate delivery will grow at the rate of interest "Rate" (here continuously compounded), less any dividends (which are also assumed to arrive continuously in tiny amounts). In the expression (Rate − Dividend) * Time, the formula nets the interest rate and the dividend income (if present) and adjusts for the amount of time for the investment. The average price in the lognormal simulation is the spot price adjusted for Rate, Dividend, and Time, as in Equation 5.7 but not including the term $\sigma^2/2$ Time.

The adjusted forward price also includes an adjustment equal to $\sigma^2/2*$ Time. The sampled values cannot go below zero for samples to the left of the adjusted forward price, and they are not bounded on the right. The log-normal distribution differs from the normal distribution, and the adjustment of $\sigma^2/2*$ Time assures that the mean of the lognormal distribution is the desired forward price.

The lognormal Monte Carlo simulation generates a random rate of return that is applied to the starting price. The first step is to create a standard normal random series (i.e., having a mean of 0 and a standard deviation of 1). Then create a sample price for each standard normal draw. Equation 5.8 applies the sample return to the standard normal random number and adjusts for the right amount of uncertainty in the pattern of returns.

$$P_i = \text{Adjusted Forward Price} * e^{N_i * \frac{\sigma}{\sqrt{\text{Time}}}} \qquad (5.8)$$

The normally distributed random number N_i is multiplied by the standard deviation. In this case, the annual standard deviation is adjusted for the time horizon Time by dividing the annual standard deviation by the square root of Time. This sample return is a continuously compounded return, so the constant e raised to the power of the sample return produces a future value factor that adjusts the starting price to become a sample price.

ADDING AND MULTIPLYING TWO RANDOM NUMBERS

When two or more normally distributed random numbers are added together, the mean and the standard deviation can be predicted in advance using formulas in standard statistics textbooks. Recall Equations 2.12 and 2.13 (repeated as Equations 5.9 and 5.10).

$$\sigma_{\text{Portfolio}} = \sqrt{w_A^2 \sigma_A^2 + 2 w_A w_B \sigma_{A,B+w_B^2 \sigma_B^2}} \qquad (5.9)$$

For N variables:

$$\sigma_{\text{Portfolio}} = \sqrt{\sum_{i=1}^{N} \sum_{j=1}^{N} w_i w_j \sigma_{i,j}} \qquad (5.10)$$

for N variables and weights of w_1 to w_N.

In trying to understand the interaction of two random variables that are added together, it may be possible to predict the sum of the two or more random variables so that a simpler Monte Carlo simulation using only one variable can sample the same uncertainty as a more complicated model. In some cases, Equations 5.9 or 5.10 can explain the uncertainty without running a simulation.

When two normally distributed random variables are multiplied together, the mean of the product of two random numbers is not equal to the product of the means of the individual random numbers, as in Equations 5.11a and 5.11b.

$$\frac{\sum_{i=1}^{N} X_i * Y_i}{N} \neq \frac{\sum_{i=1}^{N} X_i}{N} * \frac{\sum_{i=1}^{N} Y_i}{N} \tag{5.11a}$$

Or, stated more simply as the averages:

$$\overline{(X * Y)} \neq \overline{X} * \overline{Y} \tag{5.11b}$$

The standard deviation of the product cannot be predicted with simple rules. Therefore, the best way to measure the interaction between two or more random numbers is to run a simulation of the variables.

Other combinations of random numbers are possible. Suppose both the timing of a cash flow and the discount rate are uncertain. Equation 5.12 shows a mathematical statement of the present value formula based on an expected time of 10 years and an 8 percent rate.

$$PV = \frac{1,000,000}{(1 + 8\%)^{10}} = 463,193 \tag{5.12}$$

However, if the interest rate is normally distributed, with a mean of 8 percent and a standard deviation of 2 percent and the time has an expected mean of 10 years and a standard deviation of 3 years, the resulting present value averaged approximately \$485,000 with a standard deviation of \$140,000. Often, it is not clear how to estimate the combined impact of the two random processes without running a simulation.

USING RANDOM NUMBERS BUDGET IN ANALYSIS

One straightforward application of Monte Carlo simulation is to expand upon a typical sensitivity analysis conducted in a business budget. Table 5.5 represents a simple budget for a year in the future with three scenarios.

This budget contains a pessimistic scenario, a most likely scenario, and an optimistic scenario. Each case includes a forecast for net sales price and quantity sold. Expenses are budgeted to be \$60 per unit plus \$20,000,000

TABLE 5.5 Simple Annual Budget

	Sales Price	Quantity	Revenues	Expenses	Net Income
Pessimistic	80	800,000	64,000,000	68,000,000	−4,000,000
Most Likely	100	1,000,000	100,000,000	80,000,000	20,000,000
Optimistic	120	1,200,000	144,000,000	92,000,000	52,000,000

in fixed cost. Table 5.5 shows the impact of experiencing both bad pricing and poor sales, along with favorable pricing and strong sales. However, the budget does not consider a scenario in which sales prices are strong but unit sales are weak, or sales prices are weak and unit sales are strong. Further, this budget requires management to assess how likely each of these scenarios is to occur.

Table 5.6 extends the budget in Table 5.5 with Monte Carlo simulation. In this example, the sales price is uncertain but is presumed to average 100 (the most likely scenario). Unit sales are also expected to match the Most Likely scenario in Table 5.5. Fixed and variable expenses remain the same as specified in Table 5.5, running $60 per unit with an additional fixed cost of $20 million. Unlike the budget in Table 5.5, here the price is assumed to have a standard deviation of 8, presumably consistent with past patterns. Similarly, unit sales are expected to have a standard deviation of 100,000 units, again consistent with company experience.

Table 5.6 contains a condensed list of trials. The trials resulted in average income of about $20 million, matching the most likely forecast in Table 5.5. However, this analysis predicts that the standard deviation of net income is $8.65 million. Using this sensitivity information, it is possible to

TABLE 5.6 Monte Carlo Simulation of Simple Annual Budget

Trial	Sales Price	Quantity	Revenues	Expenses	Net Income
1	97.109	1,021,573	99,204,086	61,294,363	17,909,724
2	91.517	980,355	89,719,145	58,821,273	10,897,872
3	96.287	992,673	95,581,418	59,560,357	16,021,060
.	.	.	.	.	.
.	.	.	.	.	.
.	.	.	.	.	.
1,000	93.914	949,942	89,212,994	56,996,530	12,216,464
Avg	100.11	997,740	99,893,360	59,864,404	20,028,956
StDev	7.57	101,562	12,766,897	6,093,747	8,654,528

predict the chance of experience a loss. The syntax for the NORMDIST function in Excel is as follows:

$$\text{Probability of loss} = \text{NORMDIST}(0, 20028956, 8654528, \text{True})$$
$$= \text{about } 1.3\%$$

where the first input is the z value (breaking even), the second is the expected mean of 20,028,956, the third input is the standard deviation of 8,654,528, and the input of "True" tells the function to return the cumulative probabililty that the outcome will equal Z or less.

One of the three scenarios in Table 5.5 results in a loss, yet Table 5.6 suggests that there is a very small probability of experiencing a loss. Perhaps Table 5.5 is too pessimistic in combining a pessimistic forecast for both sales price and sales quantity.

Of course, Table 5.6 may be too simplistic. This solution did not account for any tendency for price surprises to be linked to quantity surprises. It is possible to generate random inputs for this budget that are correlated. Such a simulation would likely produce more extreme earnings scenarios.

In addition, the tables in this section present part of a simulation of 1,000 trials. A variety of factors affect the number of trials needed to get reliable answers. If the Monte Carlo simulation analysis produces significantly different results each time the trials are repeated, increase the number of samples.

USING RANDOM NUMBERS IN A CAPITAL BUDGETING ANALYSIS

Capital budgeting relies on net present value (NPV) analysis or internal rate of return (IRR). As part of that analysis, corporate treasurers need to consider the probability that the project will actually earn a positive NPV or an IRR above the company's required rate of return on investment projects.

Suppose one possible project required an immediate capital investment of $38 million. The project would produce cash inflows of $10 million, $12 million, $15 million, and $18 million in one, two, three, and four years, respectively. The company has a weighted average cost of capital of 14 percent. The NPV of the project is 787,558. The IRR on the project is 14.91 percent. On both accounts, the company should consider investing in the project.

Suppose that the Year 1 cash flow is expected to be $10 million, but that forecast comes with a standard deviation of $3 million. Similarly, the standard deviation of the Year 2 cash flow is $4 million. The standard

TABLE 5.7 Monte Carlo Simulation of Simple Annual Budget

	CF_1	CF_2	CF_3	CF_4	NPV	IRR
1	9,805,827	8,607,986	13,498,839	10,333,901	−7,545,001	4.24%
2	10,544,936	22,619,406	16,221,287	25,658,841	14,795,842	29.81%
.	.	.	.	.	.	.
.	.	.	.	.	.	.
.	.	.	.	.	.	.
1,000	7,244,797	15,311,598	13,029,881	28,897,228	6,041,146	20.17%
Average	9,969,005	11,790,695	15,042,984	17,822,256	523,090	14.24%
Standard Deviation	3,089,530	4,041,931	5,043,690	6,143,912	6,395,242	7.60%
				Losses	456	264
				Trials	1,000	1,000
			Sample Probability of Negative		45.60%	26.40%
		Probability of Negative NPV from Normal Distribution			46.74%	

deviation of the Year 3 cash flow is $5 million, and the standard deviation of the Year 4 cash flow is $6 million.

Table 5.7 presents a subset of trials using the mean and standard deviation of each cash flow.

The NPV and IRR are calculated from the simulated cash flows. In each case (i.e., for each row on the table), the NPV and IRR are calculated using the assumed $38 million investment and the four simulated cash flows.

As a cross check of the probability of experiencing a negative NPV, use Excel's NORMDIST(0,523090,6395242,True). The normal distribution using the sample mean and standard deviation predicts about the same probability of loss (46.74 percent) as the percent of samples (45.60 percent) actually observed and used to calculate the sample means and standard deviation.

The simulated cash flows are quite uncertain in their magnitude. The Monte Carlo simulation treats each year independently. That may be realistic for some projects and not for others. There is some averaging of year to year cash flows because of the assumptions made. Had this experiment assumed a high correlation between the four cash flows, the results from trial to trial would have varied even more.

For many projects, the near-term cash flows can be fairly precisely forecasted. Other times, there is considerable uncertainty about the success of the investment. Similarly, the later cash flows are often subject to large forecast errors. However, once a project is initiated, these later cash flows may be easier to forecast based on early results.

In any case, the project under discussion may not be a good project for investment. The scenarios show that nearly half of the time the simulated cash flows produce a negative net present value.

CONCLUSION

This chapter has introduced some tools that are used to understand uncertainty. Here, they were used to extend standard business tools such as budgets and discounted cash flow analysis.

Chapter 6 explores how a company can take advantage of this uncertainty, determine how it affects the value of potential investments, and learn how to modify projects to lower downside risk or increase upside potential.

5.1. Your city is voting on a bond issue that the local newspaper has predicted has a 75 percent chance of passing. If the referendum passes, your company has a 65 percent chance of winning the job of general contractor, a 30 percent chance of handling only the site preparation, and a 5 percent chance of getting no work. If the referendum fails, there is a 60 percent chance you will win the job of general contractor of a smaller stadium renovation project and a 40 percent chance of getting no work. Construct a tree to determine the probability of each scenario.

5.2. Use Monte Carlo simulation to estimate the chance of flipping a coin three times and coming up with heads three times?

5.3. You predict sales of 200,000 units next year. You believe that the actual sales volume is normally distributed with a standard deviation of 50,000. You have a fixed cost of $2 million and a gross margin of $15 per unit. Use Monte Carlo simulation to determine the expected gross profit. What is the chance of losing money next year?

5.4. You forecast sales equal to 100,000 units. You think there is a 25 percent chance that sales will be as low as 75,000. The sales price is also uncertain. You predict a sales price of $10 per unit, but you believe that there is a 35 percent chance that the price will be below 8. Fixed cost is $500,000 and variable costs are $4 per unit. Calculate the mean and standard deviation of gross profit.

5.5. A call gives the owner the right to buy raw materials at $100 per ton one year from now. You can buy the material now at 100 per ton, but you prefer to buy an option. Use Monte Carlo analysis to value the call assuming a 5 percent interest rate (continuously compounded) and a volatility of 15 percent (volatility is the standard deviation used for a lognormal distribution).

5.6. Create a new version of Table 5.6 from Chapter 5 in which the correlation between price and unit sales is .50.

5.7. Create two correlated normally distributed random numbers. The first series represents Project 1 and has a mean of 300,000 and a standard deviation of 250,000. Project 2 has a mean of 500,000 and a standard deviation of 500,000. The correlation between the two series is .4. Add the values together and measure the mean and standard deviation of the sum. Are the sample results roughly consistent with the theoretical mean and standard deviation determined in Questions 2.5–2.8?

Real Option Analysis of Capital Investments

INTRODUCTION

The tools developed in Chapters 1–4 are used in traditional capital budgeting to value corporate investments, securities, and government policy issues. These tools are adequate in many cases. For example, if there is relatively little uncertainty about the timing and magnitude of the cash flows (e.g., when pricing a U.S. Treasury note or bond), the capital budgeting tools are appropriate. Net present value and internal rate of return can incorporate methods to handle uncertainty. In Chapter 4, project cash flows were discounted at a company's weighted average cost of capital to account for some of the uncertainty in forecasting cash flows. The difference between the value of the cash flows discounted at a risk-free rate and the cash flows discounted at the weighted average cost of capital equals the value attached to the riskiness of the investment.

The uncertainty of the cash flows of many projects creates little problem in valuation. The net present value (NPV) of a stream of cash flows equal to $100,000 each year is mathematically equal to the net present value of a stream of cash flows that can equal either $150,000 or $50,000 (that are equally likely to occur). If that uncertainty in the second project is diversifiable, it is not even clear that the second project is less valuable or less desirable. For example, if the correlation between these annual cash flows and other corporate results is negative, the uncertain second project can materially reduce the uncertainty of overall corporate results.

Other times, the risk of a project does not fit into the NPV model very well. In Question 5.4 in Chapter 5, the reader was asked to value a call option using Monte Carlo simulation. The value of the call at expiration can never be less than zero, but it could be very valuable in some cases. In addition, scenario analysis does not capture the uncertainty unless the valuation considers a very large number of scenarios. Option pricing considers a large number of scenarios and weights each scenario according to the likelihood that it will occur.

Many projects have option-like characteristics. It stands to reason that tools from the option-pricing toolbox can be used to value such projects. Treating investment projects similarly to options has several advantages over traditional capital budgeting methods. First, the methods more adequately account for the nature of the uncertainty of cash flows associated with a project. As a result, companies will have a better way to value their investment alternatives in light of the risk posed by the alternative investment projects. Second, and potentially much more important, companies can design projects to have option-like opportunities to make projects more valuable. For example, a company can build in the opportunity to cut short an ill-fated investment and thereby limit losses on unsuccessful projects. Companies can also consider, from the outset, ways they might later react to success so as to maximize profits and include the potential for these extended profits in their initial valuation.

WHY STUDY OPTIONS?

People have been developing methods to price options for many years. Fischer Black and Myron Scholes published an important paper on this topic in 1973.* One of the unanswered questions at that time was how to value risk above and beyond the complicated problem of averaging the possible outcomes. The risk of owning a call option appeared intractable. On the one hand, a call can capture almost all the upside potential of owning a stock, but the loss is limited to the price paid to buy the call. On the other hand, call options effectively create leverage, because the price of the call is almost always less than the price of the stock. Furthermore, the chance that the option will expire worthless (because the stock ends below the strike price on the expiration date) means that an option buyer has a higher probability of very high returns and a loss of 100 percent of the money invested compared to the underlying stock.

The authors derived their call-option formula assuming that investors could maintain a position in the call and a hedging position in the underlying stock. They valued a call under the assumption that these hedges could be conducted without trading costs and commissions, that investors could

---

* Fischer Black and Myron Scholes, "The Pricing of Options and Corporate Liabilities," *Journal of Political Economy*, 81 (3), 637–654, 1973.

borrow or invest funds at a single risk-free rate, and that the uncertainty could be represented by the lognormal distribution (that distribution could be used to attach probabilities to all possible prices for the underlying stock as well as the final value of the call on the expiration date).

Black and Scholes concluded in their 1973 paper that they did not need to account specifically for the risk preferences of potential call buyers and sellers, because the main risk associated with the price of the underlying stock could be hedged. Once the model was published, a deep and broad market for many types of options and option-like securities developed—a market for instruments that had formerly been impossible to value. At the same time, researchers and traders developed many tools to value complex securities.

This chapter introduces several commonly used tools for valuing options and option-like cash flows, along with several examples of how cash flows can resemble options. In addition, this chapter gives a few examples of how investment projects can be altered to create option-like cash flows that may either limit the cost of unsuccessful investments or increase the profit of successful projects. Using these tools, companies should be able to better consider the capital investment alternatives available and to fine-tune their investing to provide the best opportunity to improve the profits of the company and maximize its share price.

WHAT IS A REAL OPTION?

The Black-Scholes call-pricing formula values an explicit option with well-documented terms and conditions. In particular, the payoff on the option is determined by the price of an asset. The original formula valued an option on a common stock, but the formula was extended to bonds, money market instruments, currencies, commodities, private equity investments, and so forth. Options on these instruments embody clearly defined rules about when the options can be exercised and when they expire.

In contrast, a real option is the value of strategic alternatives in managing a business or employing an asset. Usually, real options do not derive their value from a security or any other financial asset; the eventual value of the real option is determined by actual business success. Although the options do not have an explicit exercise provision, the payoff may be linked to some future corporate action, such as terminating an investment prematurely based on early results or additional information. In other cases, companies may split an investment in two or more phases to create an opportunity to review the investment decision and choose whether or not to make the full investment.

These real options are not new. CEOs have long considered many of the options described in this chapter when making investment and strategic decisions. Creating tools to value these considerations extends the instincts of a savvy corporate executive to the formal capital budgeting process and provides them with a means to value these considerations.

TYPES OF REAL OPTIONS

This section will identify several commonly occurring real options:

- Abandon or terminate
- Expand
- Shrink or contract
- Extend
- Make follow-on investments
- Split capital into two or more stages (staging option)

Option to Abandon or Terminate

Companies very frequently have the option to abandon or terminate unsuccessful ventures. In some cases, bankruptcy forces the decision to close. Companies routinely review the parts of the business they want to grow and the parts they want to shrink or shut down.

The innovation with real options and the option to abandon is to incorporate that predictable behavior into the initial decision to invest. The option to abandon focuses on the value of that alternative before an investment is made. The impact on investment decision-making is two-fold. First, companies may favor investment alternatives that are easy and cheap to abandon if they appear to be unsuccessful. Second, companies may design a project so that abandoning it is quick and cheap. For example, a company may outsource production of a new product even if the costs might be cheaper in-house if it can negotiate a short-term supply contract that would leave no stranded manufacturing facilities, employee termination cost, or long-term commitments to purchase raw materials.

Certainly, companies seek to invest in projects they believe will be profitable. Consumer-product companies introduce a large number of new products each year that are unsuccessful, even though the companies introducing the products must have had high hopes of success for each one. Venture capital investment funds review many, many business plans before investing in a small number of new concepts. Despite efforts to avoid unsuccessful investments, these funds make most of their return from a small number of investments. It makes sense to focus closely on the early-exit scenario at the time the company makes an investment decision.

Companies may have operations they cannot abandon. For example, a company may contract to provide a service for an extended period of time. Some operations cannot be abandoned, because doing so would impact other parts of the company too severely. It is possible that the cost to abandon may be larger than the cost of continuing a losing operation.

A company may incur significant costs if it abandons a project or business line. The company may have bought specialized equipment with limited liquidation value. Companies may even need to tear down facilities to close an operation. Companies may have expenses for pollution abatement or land reclamation. Companies likely would have severance costs and possibly litigation expenses from employee terminations. The decision to abandon should be made in light of sunk costs that may arguably be ignored and of out-of-pocket costs involved in shutting down.

Option to Expand

Investment projects may be long-lived. Sometimes a company invests in brand-new markets where the size of demand is hard to forecast. Sometimes future sales depend on the competitive response of other companies. In light of the uncertainty about required capacity, companies trade off the cost of the investment with the prospect for excess capacity. In other words, it often does not make sense to invest in enough capacity to handle the most optimistic scenario.

Often, a proposed investment requires investment in plant and equipment with a fixed maximum capacity. In the face of fixed capacity, cash flow projections may focus on the prospects for utilization at or below capacity while ignoring any chance to operate at higher levels of output. The company could later make a decision to extend capacity by making additional investments in plant and equipment or in improvements to efficiency. The option to expand considers the possibility of realizing a positive profit contribution on incremental sales.

The option to expand includes the potential value from such incremental investments at the time of the initial investment. One reason companies may not include the incremental profit from subsequent investment is that the pattern does not fit the NPV model. The opportunity to expand may be likely enough that NPV analysis includes the second investment and incremental revenues in the initial investment decision. If the probability of outsized success is smaller, then considering the potential value requires a probability-based analysis.

Option to Shrink or Contract

Just as a company may have the opportunity to increase the size of its business, it also may have the opportunity to reduce the size of a business line. The option to contract considers the possibility of capturing the profit potential by optimizing capacity to lower costs.

The option to abandon is an all-or-nothing decision. In some cases, a company may have the opportunity to reduce the size of a business. Sometimes the cost to scale back a business is small, especially if the time frame is long. Over that horizon, companies can choose not to renew leases, to reduce employment as turnover occurs, to scrap aging equipment, or to adjust product-line offerings.

Option to Extend

Companies make cash flow forecasts when considering a business investment. Many investments are finite in life, given that markets for goods change, manufacturing facilities age, competitors respond, and patents expire. Many times, however, companies can reinvest in plant and equipment, make changes in products that can extend the life of patents, rely on brands and trademarks to maintain market position after patents expire, or make other changes to extend the revenue stream.

The size and timing of these extended cash flows are uncertain, and the cost required to extend the cash flows may also be uncertain. Incorporating these incremental investments and cash inflows into the initial capital budgeting decision is possible only if the company has a basis for assessing the probability of cash inflows and outflows of various amounts.

Option to Make Follow-On Investments

Sometimes, a company enters a new market or creates a new product knowing that its first generation will earn less than the required return. Companies make these investments because the second or third generations of the product are expected to be highly profitable. Entering the business creates an option to participate in the new market with subsequent or follow-on investments.

Companies that develop new products have to deal with product life cycles. Many consumer products, such as electronics, have a very short product life. Traditional capital budgeting requires companies to quickly earn high returns from new products introduced. In many cases, however, a product becomes obsolete when a company introduces a new and better product. A company may see little profit potential in a dramatically new product because it may become obsolete before a large market develops. However, a company may still invest in the first generation to gain the opportunity to participate in second-generation and later products. Companies may be willing to accept a negative NPV product if there is a reasonably high probability that later generations of the product will produce large profits.

Staging Option

Companies considering a large investment may be able to split the capital budgeting decision into two or more stages. It may be possible to split the investment without raising the total cost of investing. For example, suppose a company is considering an investment that would require $2 million over two years and then would produce uncertain cash flows for 10 more years. If the cash flows were high, the investment would earn a sufficient return to justify investing in the project. If the cash flows were low, the investment would not earn a sufficient return.

Many times, the company can divide the investment into two or more stages. Suppose that, during the first stage, the company invests in product development to the point of producing an early version. The company can sell the product, perhaps describing it as a beta or prototype version. The company can assess the idea of a full-scale product launch based on the success of the beta launch. Note that the company may be willing to sell the beta version of the product below the price needed to earn a satisfactory return if it believes that sufficient returns could be earned on a production version of the product. In this way, the product design costs and the substandard return on the beta test can be viewed as an option premium to create an option with a payoff equal to the value of the project if the company decides to complete its phased investment in the new product.

METHODS FOR VALUING REAL OPTIONS

Scenario Analysis

You are considering investing $1.2 million now; for simplicity, assume that the entire investment occurs in equal amounts monthly at the end of each of the next 12 months. During that time, you will develop a proposed new product and conduct a beta test launch of the product. You project no revenue during the beta phase. After one year, the results of the product design and test launch will be complete. At that time, you will assess the results and make a decision whether to invest another $2 million to launch the product based on NPV analysis.

You estimate four possible scenarios based on cost studies, forecasts of unit sales, and possible pricing. You believe that there is a 15 percent chance that the first scenario will occur, yielding cash inflows worth $1,500,000 (i.e., the discounted present value, not including the $2 million investment required to roll out the product and not counting the $1.2 million in product development costs and test marketing costs; the NPV discounts cash inflows to the decision point one year from now). The second scenario carries a 35 percent chance with a predicted present value of inflows of $2,250,000 (again the present value is estimated as of one year from now and does not count the $1.2 million initial investment or the investment required to roll out the product). You estimate a 35 percent probability of the third scenario, which you would predict would provide cash flows worth $3,750,000. Finally, you forecast an optimistic scenario with a 15 percent chance you will receive cash flows worth $6 million. Should you invest in the product development if you have a weighted average cost of capital of 14 percent compounded annually?

The expected value of the scenarios and the present values of those expected values appear in Table 6.1.

The probability of the NPV of each scenario is given in the problem as stated. The NPV of each scenario includes the net of the present value of additional capital investment ($2 million) and cash inflows following that investment. The NPV is the value of the project (the investment and future cash flows) under each scenario, in each case discounted to the decision point one year from now. To consider these cash flows now, they must be discounted for an additional year. All of the NPVs are divided by $(1 + 14\%)$.

Three of the four scenarios provide a positive NPV as of one year from now, justifying a rollout of the product. That is, the $1.2 million in product development costs is a sunk cost, and the second scenario provides a positive NPV from that decision point, even though the project does not always recover the product development costs. For example, the project would

TABLE 6.1 Project Development Real Option Analysis

Scenario	Probability	Inflows	NPV	PV(NPV)
1	15%	$1,500,000	−$500,000	$0
2	35%	$2,250,000	$250,000	$219,298
3	35%	$3,750,000	$1,750,000	1,535,088
4	15%	$6,000,000	$4,000,000	3,508,722
			Current Value of Projects	$1,140,351
			Cost of Development	$1,113,746
			Value of Real Option	$26,605

return $250,000, an amount less than the $1.2 million in costs but making it worth rolling out the product to recover some of the sunk development costs.

If it becomes clear that the rollout will result in a negative NPV, the company should not proceed. Therefore, in evaluating the four alternatives, the expected value of the four scenarios involves an NPV of $0 in the first scenario and the values of the discounted NPVs in the other three scenarios.

The expected value of the four scenarios equals the probability of each scenario times the value of that scenario, as shown in the following calculation:

$$\$0 * 15\% + \$219,298 * 35\% + \$1,535,088 * 35\% + 3,508,722 * 15\%$$
$$= \$1,140,351$$

Without the real option analysis, the first scenario would be included as −$438,596 (the present value of −$500,000), and the expected value of the four scenarios would be $1,074,561.

The product development cost equals the present value of $100,000 per month discounted for 12 months at 14 percent/12. The present value of a $1 annuity was presented in Equation 4.9, reproduced here.

$$PV = \frac{1 - \dfrac{1}{(1 + \text{Rate})^N}}{\text{Rate}} \qquad (6.1)$$

Filling in the particular values,

$$PV = \frac{1 - \dfrac{1}{\left(1 + \dfrac{14\%}{12}\right)^{12}}}{\dfrac{14\%}{12}} = \$11.13746 \qquad (6.2)$$

The present value of a $100,000 annuity equals $11.13746 * $100,000 or $1,113,746.

The decision to enter into product development now is worth an expected outcome of $1,140,351 less the known product-development cost of $1,113,746. The expected value of the project now is $26,605. If the decision to roll out the product was made without consideration of the opportunity to abandon it in the first scenario, the expected value of the four scenarios, $1,074,561, would be less than the present value of the development costs of $1,113,746. Real option analysis argues for the company to assume the product development costs of $1.2 million, proceed with product development, and then decide whether to roll out the product based on the beta test.

The NPV in each scenario is forecasted prior to the product development and prior to the beta testing. Based on that testing, we can identify which one of these scenarios will apply. However, the passage of an additional year and the information gained during that year may lead to a revised forecast. In other words, the company may be able to more accurately value the particular scenario that follows the testing one year from now. The significance of that additional information cannot be determined from the example, so this scenario analysis may understate the value of the staging option.

The Black-Scholes Model

The Black-Scholes call option model values a European call (i.e., an option to buy the underlying asset on the expiration date) at a predetermined price called the strike price. The model uses the current value of the asset, the time to expiration in years, a risk-free rate of interest, and a forecasted volatility (the standard deviation of return).

Although the model was developed to value stock options, the Black-Scholes model can also value some real options. The advantage of using the Black-Scholes model is that the formula is fairly easy to value in Excel or computer programming languages and many people already have access to a program that can evaluate an option using the Black-Scholes model.

Assume that the expected value of the cash inflows is accurately described by the four scenarios presented in the previous section and that the lognormal distribution with a volatility of 15 percent can represent the probability of the outcome of the beta test. Use the Black-Scholes call formula to decide whether to proceed with the product development described in the scenario valuation of the product development problem.

Before solving the formula, we must first decide which inputs should be used in the formula. The simplest variable is the time to expiration. Although the product development process and subsequent beta testing do not require the company to adhere to a rigid expiration date, the one-year horizon in the problem provides a realistic assumption for the time to expiration. We are told to use 15 percent as the volatility assumption.

The strike price of this option is the $2 million in investment required one year from now to roll out the product. The price the company must pay for the call option is the present value of the $1.2 million cost to develop the product and test-market it. This present value was calculated as $1,113,746. The task at hand is to value this real option and decide whether it is worth buying it now for $1,113,746 (i.e., paying for the product development costs).

The interest rate is a more difficult input and real options writers do not handle the choice of rate consistently. The Black-Scholes model presumes that a hedge can be created between the call (in this case, the real option) and the underlying asset (the NPV one year from now following the beta test). If this hedge was possible to construct, the proper rate would be a risk-free rate (possibly the yield on 1-year U.S. Treasury bills). This hedge, of course, cannot be constructed, because the company cannot buy or sell the project on a securities exchange and there is no way to hedge the success or failure of the product development and beta test launch.

This analysis uses a discount rate of 14 percent compounded annually, assuming that this project is as risky as the other projects the company has invested in (i.e., that the company's weighted average cost of capital is the right rate to compensate for the risk in this project that cannot be hedged).

However, the Black-Scholes model requires an interest rate that is continuously compounded. To convert the 14 percent annual rate to continuous compounding, take the natural log of the future value of the annually compounded rate (ln(1.14) = 13.103 percent). The continuously compounded rate of 13.103 percent is equivalent to a 14 percent annually compounded rate.

Determining the value of the underlying asset in the formula (S in the original Black-Scholes formula and Spot in Equation 6.4 representing the current value of the underlying stock) is a tricky matter. The Black-Scholes model uses this input to center the lognormal distribution around the forward price of the stock. To set up this real option problem correctly, the value must be the input that centers the forward value of future revenues around the proper value. Stated differently, we need to instruct the model where to place the mean of the lognormal distribution of possible revenue projections. The proper forward value is the expected value of the Inflows values of the four scenarios shown in Table 6.1. These values are not present value adjusted and should not be. The expected value of the Inflows values under the four scenarios is

$$\$1,500,000 * 15\% + \$2,250,000 * 35\% + \$3,750,000 * 35\% \\ + 6,000,000 * 15\% = \$3,225,000 \quad (6.3)$$

However, Black-Scholes assumes that a zero-dividend stock rises at the short-term rate (14 percent annually or 13.104 percent continuous), so the input for S is $3,225,000 discounted for a year at 13.104 percent; $3,225,000 times e to the power of -13.104 percent gives $2,828,947 for the input Spot.

The next step is to calculate d_1 and d_2.

$$d_1 = \frac{ln\left(\dfrac{Spot}{Strike}\right) + \left(Rate + \dfrac{\sigma^2}{2}\right) * Time}{\sigma\sqrt{Time}} \qquad (6.4)$$

where ln refers to the natural logarithm function, $\sqrt{}$ is the square root function, Spot is the present value of the expected value of the expected future cash flows (not including the follow-on investment), Strike is the amount of the follow-on investment, Time is the time until the decision whether to make the follow-on investment should be made, Rate is the appropriate discount rate for that period of time, and σ (sigma) is the parameter used to attach probabilities to various values of the present value of future cash flows.

The formula for d_1 in Excel would look like the following cell formula.

$$= (ln(2828947/2000000) + ((13.104\% + 15\% * 15\%/2) * 1))/15\%/(1\wedge 0.5) \qquad (6.5)$$

The value for d_1 equals 3.260.

$$d_2 = d_1 - \sigma\sqrt{Time} \qquad (6.6)$$

The formula for d_2 in Excel would look like the following cell formula:

$$= 3.260 - 15\% * (1\wedge 0.5) \qquad (6.7)$$

The value for d_2 equals 3.110.

Next, calculate the probability for d_1 and d_2 using the cumulative normal distribution. The NORMSDIST function in Excel can calculate this probability, as follows:

For $N(d_1)$

$$= NORMSDIST(3.260) \qquad (6.8)$$

The value for $N(d_1)$ is 0.999.
For $N(d_2)$

$$= NORMSDIST(3.110) \qquad (6.9)$$

The value for $N(d_2)$ is 0.999.
Finally, apply the Black-Scholes call option formula:

$$c = Spot * N(d_1) - Strike * N(d_2) * e^{-Rate*Time} \qquad (6.10)$$

$$c = 2,828,947 * 0.999 - 2,000,000 * .999 * .877 = 1,074,627 \quad (6.11)$$

This valuation shows that the option to invest $2 million one year from now to roll out a new product is worth $1,074,627, which is less than the cost of $1,113,746. The company would be advised against pursuing the product development.

The Black-Scholes model does not produce the same conclusion as the scenario analysis, nor does it make specific assumptions about a limited number of scenarios. Instead, it values a continuous range of assumptions. The Black-Scholes model includes the four scenarios along with numerous other scenarios. Black-Scholes attaches a low probability to any particular scenario. For example, the model attaches a low probability of revenues totaling $6 million with a net present value of $4 million, but it also includes a probability for revenues of $5.99 million and $6.01 million and countless other alternatives.

The Binomial Option Pricing Model

You are considering an investment that would require an investment of $50 million now. The investment would produce expected annual gross revenues of $10 million per year (there are no noncash revenues and expenses on the income statement), with fixed costs of $2.5 million per year. The project would last 10 years and the equipment would have no salvage value. However, at the end of each of the 10 years, you could close the operation, sell the equipment for approximately the straight-line depreciated book value, and avoid additional fixed charges.

Use a binomial tree with 15 percent annual volatility to value the project in light of the option to abandon. The risk-free rate is 4 percent and the company's cost of capital is 14 percent.

Before beginning, notice that the project has a negative net present value using traditional capital budgeting tools. The present value of the 10 annual cash flows of $7.5 million ($10 million operating profit less $2.5 million fixed cost) is worth $39.12 million, discounted at the 14 percent. The projected cash flows do not justify making a $50 million investment.

The binomial option pricing model defines a couple of parameters necessary to build the tree. The tree in this example is built annually, although more accurate values are possible if the analysis were made with more frequent valuation points. At each node in the tree, the gross revenue can go up or down only one standard deviation so that the tree prices are consistent with 15 percent volatility. Therefore, the beginning gross income can go up to $11.62 million ($10 * e^{15\%} = 11.62$) or down to

1	2	3	4	5	6	7	8	9	10
									44.82
								38.57	
							33.20		33.20
						28.58		28.58	
					24.60		24.60		24.60
				21.17		21.17		21.17	
			18.22		18.22		18.22		18.22
		15.68		15.68		15.68		15.68	
	13.50		13.50		13.50		13.50		13.50
11.62		11.62		11.62		11.62		11.62	
10.00	10.00		10.00		10.00		10.00		10.00
8.61		8.61		8.61		8.61		8.61	
	7.41		7.41		7.41		7.41		7.41
		6.38		6.38		6.38		6.38	
			5.49		5.49		5.49		5.49
				4.72		4.72		4.72	
					4.07		4.07		4.07
						3.50		3.50	
							3.01		3.01
								2.59	
									2.23

FIGURE 6.1 Tree of Gross Revenues

$8.61 million (10 $* e^{-15\%}$ = 8.61). As a shortcut, note that each move up will be 1.162 times the starting price (often called u) and each move down will be .861 times the starting price (often called d). The table of possible levels for gross revenue appears as Figure 6.1.

Figure 6.2 reduces all of the values in Figure 6.1 by the fixed costs. These values constitute a range of annual cash flows on the investment.

The binomial option pricing model defines the probability of moving up as

$$p = \frac{e^{\text{Rate}*\text{Time}} - d}{u - d} \qquad (6.12)$$

Using 4 percent interest rate and the previously calculated values for u and d, Equation 6.12 becomes 6.13.

$$p = \frac{e^{4\%*\text{Time}} - e^{-\sigma*\sqrt{\text{Time}}}}{e^{\sigma*\sqrt{\text{Time}}} - e^{-\alpha*\sqrt{\text{Time}}}} = \frac{1.041 - .861}{1.162 - .861} = 59.81\% \qquad (6.13)$$

The probability of moving down is $1 - p$, or 40.19 percent.

	1	2	3	4	5	6	7	8	9	10
										42.32
									36.07	
								30.70		30.70
							26.08		26.08	
						22.10		22.10		22.10
					18.67		18.67		18.67	
				15.72		15.72		15.72		15.72
			13.18		13.18		13.18		13.18	
		11.00		11.00		11.00		11.00		11.00
	9.12		9.12		9.12		9.12		9.12	
7.50		7.50		7.50		7.50		7.50		7.50
	6.11		6.11		6.11		6.11		6.11	
		4.91		4.91		4.91		4.91		4.91
			3.88		3.88		3.88		3.88	
				2.99		2.99		2.99		2.99
					2.22		2.22		2.22	
						1.57		1.57		1.57
							1.00		1.00	
								0.51		0.51
									0.09	
										−0.27

FIGURE 6.2 Tree of Net Cash Flows

The tree in Figure 6.3 values the cash flows, discounting each cash flow one year at a time at 4 percent and applying the probabilities to work from right to left on the tree. In the final year, the starting value is the salvage value of the equipment (here assumed to be zero). Then, for each prior year, the value of each element on the tree is the present value of the expected value of the later cash flows plus the immediate cash flow. However, if the value of the node becomes less than the book value of the equipment, the tree includes that higher liquidation value at that node (see Figure 6.3).

The value in the tenth column is the greater of the present value of all subsequent cash flows (zero because there are no more cash flows) and the salvage value (in this case, also zero). To calculate the top value in the ninth column ($36.20 million), sum the cell up one row and to the right one column on Table 6.3 plus the corresponding cash flow on Table 6.2 and weight by the probability of an up move ((0 + 42.32 million) * 59.81 percent). Also sum the cell down one row and to the right one column on Table 6.3 plus the corresponding cash flow on Table 6.2 and weight by the probability of a down move ((0 + 30.70) million * 40.19 percent). Add the two values and discount at 4 percent for a year. Finally, compare the calculated value with

	1	2	3	4	5	6	7	8	9	10
										0.00
									36.20	
								61.76		0.00
							78.93		26.19	
						89.50		44.53		0.00
					94.97		56.67		18.78	
				96.52		63.95		31.77		0.00
			95.12		67.47		40.19		13.29	
		91.57		68.12		45.92		22.31		0.00
	86.55		66.66		47.12		27.97		9.22	
80.70		63.82		47.26		31.06		15.31		0.00
	60.36		46.28		32.49		19.08		6.21	
		45.15		33.36		21.78		10.51		0.00
			35.00		25.00		15.00		5.00	
				30.00		20.00		10.00		0.00
					25.00		15.00		5.00	
						20.00		10.00		0.00
							15.00		5.00	
								10.00		0.00
									5.00	
										0.00

FIGURE 6.3   Valuation Tree

the salvage value of the assets ($5 million in Year 9). The value of the project at this point is the greater of the calculated value (the ongoing value of the business) and the salvage value.

Calculate each entry on Table 6.3 similarly. The value on the binomial tree is $80.70, which is greater than the investment of $50 million. The investment has a positive option value, because the chance of significant improvements in gross revenue adds to the value of the project; in addition, the ability to sell the equipment and avoid net losses reduces the downside risk.

Monte Carlo Simulation

Both the Black-Scholes model and the binomial pricing model are fairly inflexible and somewhat difficult to use. In contrast, Monte Carlo simulation is quite flexible. The following scenario shows the importance of handling uncertainty and includes a simple example that values the option to expand.

You are considering building a plant to manufacture a new product. The plant will cost $1.250 million to build, and for simplicity, assume that that payment would occur immediately. You will be able to build and sell up to 10,000 units per year for 10 years, after which the plant will be obsolete and have no net salvage value. Assume that you can sell the product for $125 per unit and that you have variable costs of $50 per unit plus a fixed cost of $500,000 per year. Again, for simplicity, assume no inflation in costs or sales price. Discount net income using a 12 percent Weighted Average Cost of Capital.

This is a standard textbook capital budgeting example. At 10,000 units per year, the plant will generate $125 * 10,000 or $1,250,000 in revenue per year. Costs at that level of activity are $500,000 fixed cost plus $50 * 10,000 or $1,000,000. The net present value of the investment is the value of a 10-year ordinary annuity less the investment.

Using Equation 4.9 (reproduced below as Equation 6.14) with inputs from the investment problem previously stated, the value of the net cash flow is:

$$PV = 250,000 * \frac{1 - \frac{1}{(1 + 12\%)^{10}}}{12\%} \qquad (6.14)$$

The value of the 10 cash inflows equals $1,412,556. The net present value is $162,556. Alternatively, the investment has an internal rate of return equal to 15.10 percent. Based on traditional capital budgeting, the company should make the investment.

Suppose, however, that there is some uncertainty about how many units you will sell. You believe that sales will be flat for each of the next 10 years. You forecast an average sales volume of 10,000 units, but a standard deviation of 2,500 units reflects your uncertainty about the actual sales number.

The Monte Carlo simulation created 1,000 sales trials that averaged close to the expected level of 10,000 units per year. The standard deviation of unit sales was also close to 2,500 units. As previously, revenues reflect the units times $125 sales price, but revenue is different for each level of sampled unit sales. The expenses equal the fixed cost of $500,000 plus $50 per unit. Net income, therefore, reflects the impact of uncertain unit sales on both revenues and expenses. Finally, the far-right column in Table 6.2 calculates the net present value of each trial by assuming the same sales will persist for 10 years. The net present value discounts the net income and subtracts the initial investment of $1.25 million.

Unlike the nonrandom case, Table 6.2 reflects potential sales that are significantly above or below 10,000, even though the average of potential units sales approximately equals 10,000. However, Table 6.2 assumes that the capacity equals exactly 10,000. If potential sales are 10,000 or less, the company can make and sell the number of units desired by customers.

TABLE 6.2 Monte Carlo Simulation of Sales Levels

	Potential Sales	Actual Sales	Revenue	Expense	Net Income	NPV
	9,249	9,249	1,156,177	962,471	193,706	−$155,515
	6,806	6,806	850,724	840,290	10,434	−1,191,043
	10,611	10,000	1,250,000	1,000,000	250,000	162,556
	.	.	.	.	.	
	.	.	.	.	.	
	.	.	.	.	.	
	9,344	9,344	1,167,967	967,187	200,780	−115,547
Maximum	17,539	10,000	1,250,000	250,000	162,556	
Minimum	3,076	3,076	384,548	653,819	−269,271	−2,771,444
Mean	10,063	8,992	1,124,035	949,614	174,421	−264,482
Standard deviation	2,553	1,439	179,831	71,932	107,899	609,652

If customers desire more than 10,000 units, the company is limited to making and selling 10,000 units.

This uncertainty significantly reduces the attractiveness of the investment. Because the company suffers from reduced sales if potential sales are below 10,000 but does not benefit when potential sales are above 10,000, the average is below the potential. For the 1,000 samples drawn, the average trial allowed the company to sell 8,992 units. This lower level of sales reduced the average net income from $250,000 (the annual income at the maximum possible output) to $174,421, producing a negative net present value of $264,482. Further, over 40 percent of the trials resulted in negative NPV.

This example is a bit simplistic. Perhaps the company would have sales that vary from year to year. In that case, the company could inventory production in slow years to sell in later years. More importantly, the company could take steps to increase capacity.

Suppose the company negotiated a supply agreement with an outside manufacturer to produce up to 10,000 more units at a cost of $80 per unit. Because the company would make less per unit on these outsourced units, it would always produce and sell its own units first. However, even though the company would keep a smaller gross margin per unit, it would benefit by making more sales.

Table 6.3 extends the Monte Carlo simulation in Table 6.2 using the same sampled unit sales. The revenue equals $125 per unit times the number of potential sales. However, the company can now sell up to 20,000 units, more than this particular simulation encountered. Expenses for internally manufactured units equal $500,000 plus $50 per unit times the

TABLE 6.3 Monte Carlo Simulation of the Option to Expand

	Potential Sales	Internal Units	Extra Units	Revenue	Expense	Net Income	NPV
	9,249	9,249	0	1,156,177	962,471	193,706	−$155,515
	6,806	6,806	0	850,724	840,290	10,434	−1,191,043
	10,611	10,000	611	1,326,330	1,000,000	250,000	317,818
	.	.	.	.	.	.	
	.	.	.	.	.	.	
	.	.	.	.	.	.	
	9,344	9,344	0	1,167,967	967,187	200,780	−115,547
Max	17,539	10,000	7,539	2,192,418	1,603,148	5898,271	2,079,510
Min	3,076	3,076	0	384,548	653,819	−269,271	−2,771,444
Mean	10,063	8,992	1,070	1,257,833	1,035,244	222,588	7,673
St. Dev.	2,553	1,439	1,512	319,088	168,671	153,498	867,300

number of potential sales, up to a maximum of 10,000 units. The cost of sales of incremental units above 10,000 internally produced units equals $80 per unit with no fixed cost.

The option to expand incorporates the scenario that the company experiences significantly higher sales than projected and that the company can make provisions to expand capacity to take advantage of the strong demand. In the example above, the company can sell more products than their internal capacity by outsourcing incremental production. The uncertainty about sales may make an investment in that peak capacity unprofitable unless sales are stronger than forecasted. However, the ability to capture some of the benefit of this strong demand allows the company to value the prospect of this outcome into their investment decision.

CONCLUSION

Real option analysis applies the knowledge learned from the growth of the derivative markets to the capital budgeting problem. The opportunity to quantify important business opportunities and incorporate the value that can be created (or losses that can be avoided) increases the value of projects at the time the company is considering the investment.

The information may permit companies to accept investment projects they otherwise would reject without real-option analysis. More importantly, armed with the knowledge of real options, managers can create the opportunity to produce higher returns for shareholders.

6.1. Calculate the Black-Scholes call value from the information provided in Question 5.5.

Day Counting for Interest Rate Calculations

INTRODUCTION

Chapter 1 introduces the concepts of present value and future value. The future value is linked to the present value by an interest rate and the length of time. The analysis requires the proper interest rate. The compounding frequency may significantly affect the results. The way time is measured can also affect the link between present value and future value. To fully understand how to use any interest rate in present-valuing calculations, the user must know the assumptions to make regarding day counting.

Most of the methods described herein as well as additional variations can be divided between two general strategies. One method, often called the "actual" method, spreads the annual interest rate equally over each day in the period (which could be a yearly, a semiannual, or a quarterly coupon payment). Some years have 365 days, and others have 366 days. Some semiannual periods have 181 days, and others have 184 days. Months can have between 28 and 31 days.

The second method, often called the "30/360" method, spreads the annual interest rate equally over 12 months. Under this method, the same amount of interest (one-twelfth of the annual rate) is paid in February (which has 28 or 29 days) and March (which has 31 days).

The day-counting method can significantly affect the present value or future value calculations over short periods of time. In practice, interest rates adjust to short cash periods that include a February month-end or a month-end for months with 31 days.

THE 30/360 METHOD

The 30/360 method assumes that each month has 30 days and each year has 360 days. Because of this simplifying assumption, interest could be readily calculated from preprinted tables. This simplification was convenient before computers and calculators became readily available.

The 30/360 method is commonly used despite the availability of computers to incorporate more information about the calendar into interest calculations. Most U.S. corporate and municipal bonds use the 30/360 method as do a large number of loan documents and many derivative contracts.

If an interest period corresponds to a calendar month, the interest using the 30/360 method is simply the annual interest on the balance divided by 12. Frequently, interest periods run from a particular date in one month to the same date in the next month. This period also earns 30 days of interest. For example, the day count from February 15 to March 15 may have 28 or 29 actual days but the period receives 30 days of interest, or one-twelfth of the annual rate.

Periods less than a month may be paid based on the actual number of days. For example, the 20 actual days from the 5th day of the month to the 25th day of the same month would receive 20/30 of the monthly rate (one-twelfth of the annual rate).

In general, periods that extend beyond a month each receive (30 less the starting date) days of interest for the balance of time in the month. Then, the rate applies for 30 more days for each complete month to follow. Finally, the rate applies to the end date in the ending month (for example, count 14 days more if the rate period ends on the 14th day of the month).

A general method simplifies the count of days using the 30/360 calendar. Suppose the starting date is MM1/DD1/YY1 and the ending date is MM2/DD2/YY2. The 30/360 day count has three parts.

$$\text{Days}_{30/360} = 360 * (YY2 - YY1) + 30 * (MM2 - MM1) + DD2 - DD1$$

Start with the number of years between the starting date and the ending date times 360. If the calendar year of the start of the period is the same as the year of the end of the period, this value is zero. In other cases, the formula adds 360 days for each year in the holding period.

The second term is the number of months between the starting date and the ending date times 30. This adjustment could increase the day count if the month of the ending date is later in the year than the month of the beginning date. Alternatively, the second term could decrease the day count if the month of the ending date is earlier in the ending year than the month of the beginning date in the year the period begins.

The third term adjusts the day count for the day of the month of the starting date compared with the day of the month of the ending date.

Several assumptions must be made in particular circumstances. In particular, if the starting date is the end of the calendar month, it is common to treat the starting date as though it occurred on the 30th day of the month. In some cases, market participants treat a date on the 31st of a month as though it occurred on the first day of the next month.

THE ACTUAL/ACTUAL METHOD

Perhaps the most intuitive day-counting method is to count the actual number of days. Most computer environments can calculate the actual number of days between two dates. This actual day count provides a basis for present value discounting and for calculating interest expense.

Often, interest rates are prorated over an entire year. In this case, each day counts equally in the present-valuing process, and interest accrues equally each day of the year. In this case, each day counts as either 1/365 or 1/366. Whether to include the extra leap day depends on the year in question (usually not the calendar year). Years that do not contain February 29 are assumed to have 365 days. Years that do contain February 29 are assumed to have 366 days.

Semiannual interest rates are usually allocated first to a particular 6-month period then to individual days. For example, a 6 percent annual rate would pay 3 percent each semiannual period. Within each period, the income or expense may be allocated based on the actual days in the coupon period. For most semiannual periods, the length of the period is either 181 days or 184 days in years with 365 days. An extra day for February 29 may lengthen the semiannual period.

Under the actual/actual method, the semiannual rate is applied evenly over the days in the period. As a result, the present value and future value equations use a lower daily rate for periods having 184 days than for periods having 181 days.

THE ACTUAL/360 METHOD

Some fixed-income instruments use 360 for the assumed number of days in the year but count the actual number of days in the present-valuing period. For example, a 3-month money market investment may have 91 days between purchase and maturity. The fraction 91/360 measures the fraction of the annual rate to use for present value and future value calculations, rather than 91/365 (using actual/actual) or 90/360 (using 30/360).

One impact of the actual/360 method is to raise the effective interest rate slightly. This rate may be adjusted by multiplying a quoted actual/360 rate by 365/360. This adjustment incrementally raises the interest rate to more closely approximate the real cost of interest.

THE ACTUAL/365 METHOD

The actual/365 method is similar to the actual/actual method. Under the actual/365 method, all years are assumed to have exactly 365 days. The period of time from the beginning of a period to its end is stated in years as the actual number of days in the period divided by 365.

The method does not adjust for years that contain an extra day. Therefore, the measure of time in years containing February 29 still divides the actual number of days by 365.

The actual/365 method creates slightly higher time intervals for long-dated cash flows, because the impact of missing days affects the measure of time in years.

EXAMPLE AND COMPARISON OF 30/360 AND ACTUAL/ACTUAL

Suppose you need to calculate the future value of a $10,000,000 cash flow from February 27, 2007 to March 1, 2007, a year that does not have an extra day in February. February 27 is not the last day of the month. Your bank offers to lend money at 3 percent. The loan requires you to put up collateral (government securities you already own). The bank uses 30/360 day counting. Alternatively, you could liquidate some of the investments and use the proceeds for the short-term liquidity needs. These investments yield 5 percent (based on actual/actual day counting).

The bank loan would charge four days of interest, not two. This example is admittedly an extreme example but one that actually happens, and the bank quoted rate reflects the quirky day counting. The interest is $10 million * 3% * 4/360 or $3,333. The future value is $10,003,333 using a 3 percent interest rate and a time of 4/360 or .011.

By selling the government securities, the company loses the 5 percent investment return (and perhaps a bit more if the company paid transaction costs to sell the position). U.S. Treasury securities use the actual number of days between February 27 and March 1, which is two. There are 365 days in this year. Using the actual number of days and the 5 percent opportunity cost, the imputed interest is $10 million * 5 percent * 2/365 or $2,740. The forward value of $10 million is $10,002,740 using a 5 percent interest rate and a time of 2/365 or .0055. The cheapest source of funds is to sell the government securities and forgo the 5 percent return, rather than pay a quoted rate of 3 percent to the bank.

If this scenario were to be repeated in 2008, which is a leap year, the results would differ. The company now can borrow $10 million at 3 percent from February 27, 2008 to March 1, 2008. The bank would still charge four days of interest or $3,333. The future value is still $10,003,333 based on the quoted rate of 3 percent and a time of 4/360 or .011.

The sale of the government securities now causes the company to forgo the 5 percent return for three actual days. The implicit cost is $10 million * 5 percent * 3/366 or $4,098. The forward value of $10 million is $10,004,098 using a 5 percent interest rate and a time of 3/366, or .0055. The cheapest source of funds is the bank loan at 3 percent, even though it will lead to an interest expense that charges for four days of interest.

IMPACT OF DAY COUNTING OVER LONGER INTERVALS

The impact of a day-counting assumption is largest for certain short time intervals involving periods that extend over month-end. Table A.1 lists a series of dates beginning on February 27, 2007 and the future value of $10 million, using both the actual/actual and the 30/360 methods of day counting along with 5 percent simple interest.

These results demonstrate that the difference between these two day-counting methods persists to some degree for longer periods of time. In fact, the difference is generally not zero beyond one year. Because of these differences, quoted interest rates reflect the impact of these day-counting assumptions. To correctly include the market level of interest rates into the time value of money adjustment, this present valuing should reflect the day-counting method that is consistent with the market rates in use.

CALCULATING CALENDAR INTERVALS OVER LONG PERIODS

The day-counting routines described in this appendix are frequently used only for the first recurring period. After the first payment date, the time interval is deemed to be longer, based on the coupon frequency.

TABLE A.1 Future Value of $10 Million Beginning February 27, 2007 Deviation of Return

Date	Actual/365	30/360	Interest % Difference
3/1/07	$10,002,740	$10,005,556	102.8%
3/31/07	$10,043,836	$10,047,222	7.7%
4/30/07	$10,084,932	$10,077,500	3.0%
5/31/07	$10,127,397	$10,130,556	2.5%
6/30/07	$10,168,493	$10,170,833	1.4%
7/31/07	$10,210,959	$10,213,889	1.4%
8/31/07	$10,253,425	$10,255,556	0.8%
9/30/07	$10,294,521	$10,295,833	0.4%
10/31/07	$10,336,986	$10,338,889	0.6%
11/30/07	$10,378,082	$10,379,167	0.3%
12/31/07	$10,420,548	$10,422,222	0.4%
1/31/08	$10,463,014	$10,463,889	0.2%
2/29/08	$10,502,740	$10,502,778	0.0%

For example, the day-counting assumptions for a semiannual bond coupon are used for the first period. This bond may have a fractional period remaining until the first semiannual coupon is paid. The exact length of this period will reflect the day-counting convention for the bond. Each coupon following is deemed to arrive exactly .5 years later than the previous payment.

This assumption is very convenient, because all the coupon payments can be priced using the annuity formula introduced in Chapter 4. As a result, however, the yield of a bond reflects this convention, not just the timing of individual cash flows using one of the day counting conventions mentioned earlier. In most cases, the impact of the timing is small.

A NOTE ABOUT CONTINUOUS COMPOUNDING

Academic articles often make time value adjustments using continuous compounding. Often, the continuously compounded formula for present or future value simplifies equations. Many market practitioners also convert rates that use different compounding frequencies and different day-counting conventions to equivalent continuously compounded rates. The practice can help to ensure that all discounting is consistent with the conventions of the interest rates used as inputs.

CONCLUSION

The day-counting convention is a complication that stems at least in part from the shortcuts that were used in lending markets before the market participants had ready access to precise ways to determine interest. Idiosyncrasies involving these methods are well known to market participants. To properly determine the present value or future value of a cash flow, it is important to seek out market interest rates and apply the rates mindful of the compounding frequency and day-counting practices used by market participants.

Questions and Answers

INTRODUCTION

The review questions for each chapter cover key concepts that are often incorporated in the main body of a finance textbook. In this book, the chapters are short by design, but the answers to questions delve more deeply into these key concepts. Where possible, these answers provide several ways to use the concepts presented in the text to value cash flows and projects.

CHAPTER 1

1.1 Your supplier asks you to pay your $300,000 invoice in 30 days. However, the supplier will allow you to pay $298,500 immediately. You can borrow at 5 percent (annual rate). Should you pay $298,500 immediately or $300,000 in 30 days? Ignore any impact of taxes.

Answer:

Pay $298,500 now.

Suppose you would need to borrow the entire $298,500 to make an immediate payment. Making the assumption that the company will borrow the entire amount is a convenient technique in finance. Because the company fully replaces the cash used to make the early payment, the transaction is fully financed. As long as the comparison between the two cash flows includes the cost of the loan, the comparison also includes the costs affected by the timing of the cash flow.

The early payment plus a 30-day bank loan is sometimes called a replicating portfolio. That is, these two business transactions together act identically to the delayed payment of $300,000. Because they act the same, they should be worth the same.

The first alternative is to pay $298,500, by borrowing $298,500 and repaying the loan with interest 30 days later. The second alternative is to make no cash payment immediately and pay $300,000 in 30 days.

Both strategies require no net cash payment immediately and a single cash flow 30 days later. The comparison requires a measure of interest: 298,500 * 5 percent/12 = $1,243.75. The company must repay the bank $298,500 + $1,243.75 or $299,743.75. This alternative, which involves early payment of the smaller amount plus interest, is less expensive than a payment of $300,000.

The two cash flows can be compared because the immediate payment is converted to a future value. Note that these tools are usually used to discount all cash flows to the present. This typical practice requires a slightly different description of the replicating portfolio.

The first alternative is to pay $298,500 immediately. The second alternative is to invest a certain cash amount immediately at a 5 percent interest rate and then to redeem the investment and pay $300,000 in 30 days.

Of course, the immediate payment of $298,500 is already equal to the present value of the immediate cash payment. The alternative for the company is to deposit enough money to create exactly $300,000 in 30 days. Assuming that money will earn 5 percent,

$$PV * \left(1 + \frac{5\%}{12}\right) = 300,000$$

Move the interest rate term to the right-hand side and apply the known values.

$$PV = \frac{300,000}{1 + \dfrac{5\%}{12}} = 298,755.19$$

As with the future value comparison, the present value of the immediate payment ($298,500) is less than the present value of a payment one month later ($298,755.19). The cheaper alternative is to pay the lower invoice amount immediately.

1.2 Ignoring any impact of taxes, what borrowing rate would make you indifferent between paying the invoice in Question 1.1 immediately and paying $300,000 in a month?

Answer:

The company should be indifferent if the present values of the two cash flows are equal.

$$PV = \frac{FV}{1 + \dfrac{Rate}{12}}$$

Move the denominator to the left-hand side.

$$PV\left(1 + \frac{Rate}{12}\right) = FV$$

Multiply the PV and the two values within the parentheses to remove the parentheses.

$$PV + PV\frac{Rate}{12} = FV$$

Subtract PV from both sides to move one PV term to the right.

$$PV\frac{Rate}{12} = FV - PV$$

Finally, solve for the rate.

$$Rate = \frac{(FV - PV)}{PV} * 12 = \frac{(300,000 - 298,500)}{298,500} * 12 = 6.03.\%$$

The final equation used to find the rate should make intuitive sense to the reader. The difference between 300,000 and 298,500 is an implicit interest expense for deferring payment 30 days. The $298,500 is the principal amount of the financing transaction. The ratio of (300,000 less 298,500) to 298,500 is a simple rate of return. Since the simple return occurs over one month, the annual rate is 12 times larger. This rate is compounded monthly.

1.3a If you deposit money today into an account that pays 6.5 percent interest, how long will it take you to double your money if interest does not compound (simple interest)?

Answer:

Simple interest earns no interest on interest, so the deposit doubles when interest equals the initial principal (Prin). That interest equals the annual rate (Rate) times the length of time the return accumulates (Years).

$$2 * Prin = Prin + Prin * Rate_{Simple} * Years$$

Divide each side of the equation above by Prin.

$$2 = 1 + Rate_{Simple} * Years$$

Subtract 1 from each side.

$$1 = \text{Rate}_{\text{Simple}} * \text{Years}$$

Divide each side by $\text{Rate}_{\text{Simple}}$, which is 6.5 percent.

$$\text{Years} = \frac{1}{\text{Rate}_{\text{Simple}}} = \frac{1}{6.5\%} = 15.385$$

1.3b If interest compounds annually?
Answer:

$$2 * \text{Principal} = \text{Principal}(1 + \text{Rate}_{\text{Annual}})^{\text{Years}}$$

A strategy follows to determine the exact number of years for semiannual and quarterly compounding. For this annually compounded example, consider a well-known approximation. The Rule of 72 provides a rough estimate of the number of years it takes to double an investment at 6.5 percent. According to this approximation, 72 divided by the interest rate approximately equals the number of years required to double. In this case, 72 divided by 6.5 (note that the rule uses a numerical value for the rate that is 100 times greater than the equivalent decimal of .065). This approximation equals 11.077, an approximation that is actually very close to the actual years of 11.007.

1.3c If it compounds semiannually?
Answer:
The investment doubles when compounded interest raises the value of the account to double the initial investment.

$$2 * \text{Prin} = \text{Prin}\left(1 + \frac{\text{Rate}_{\text{Semiannual}}}{2}\right)^{2*\text{Years}}$$

where $\text{Rate}_{\text{Semiannual}}$ is an annualized return that compounds semiannually. For example, a 6.5 percent semiannual rate would earn 3.25 percent over the first semiannual period and that return would earn interest at 3.25 percent over the second semiannual period.

The natural logarithm function can be used as a first step to find the rate.

$$\ln(2) = \ln\left(1 + \frac{\text{Rate}_{\text{Semiannual}}}{2}\right) * 2 * \text{Years}$$

The natural logarithm function (or the logarithm using any base) affects the value of the two constants, 2 and the expression involving rate (which reduces to 1.0325 in this particular case) and creates a relationship that can be solved for Years.

$$\text{Years} = \frac{\ln(2)}{2 * \ln\left(1 + \dfrac{\text{Rate}_{\text{Semiannual}}}{2}\right)} = \frac{\ln(2)}{2 * \ln\left(1 + \dfrac{6.5\%}{2}\right)} = 10.836$$

1.3d If interest compounds quarterly?
Answer:
Quarterly compounding follows the same procedure as demonstrated for semiannual compounding:

$$\text{Years} = \frac{\ln(2)}{4 * \ln\left(1 + \dfrac{\text{Rate}_{\text{Quarterly}}}{4}\right)} = \frac{\ln(2)}{4 * \ln\left(1 + \dfrac{6.5\%}{4}\right)} = 10.750$$

where $\text{Rate}_{\text{Quarterly}}$ is an annualized return that compounds four times each year. For example, a 6.5 percent quarterly rate would earn 1.625 percent over the first quarter and that return would earn interest at 1.625 percent over the next quarter.

Excel makes available a handy tool that can be used to determine the number of years in each of these variations. To use Goal Seek to calculate the number of years to double an investment at a 6.5 percent quarterly compounded rate of return, first store a guess for the number of years to break even in an Excel cell. Next, program a second cell with the formula for future value, relying on the years in the first cell. For example, suppose you entered 10.1 in cell A1. Then, in cell B1, you enter "= 1 * (1 + 6.5%/4)^(4 * A1)."

Cell B1 will return 1.918, not quite double the initial present value. Changing the years in A1 to 11 causes the future value in B1 to grow to 2.032. The investment doubles slightly before the end of 11 years. The exact time when the investment doubles can be found by trial and error.

Excel's Goal Seek function can perform the trial and error search. To access the utility from Office 2007, click on the DATA/WHAT-IF-ANALYSIS menu and select GOAL SEEK. Then fill in the three inputs:
Set cell: "B1"
To value: enter the number "2" in the box
By changing cell: enter "A1"

Goal Seek will find that the value 10.751 produces a value of 2 in cell B2. This is not an exact answer but is as close as Goal Seek got to 2 before exiting the search. The value differs only slightly from the exact answer of 10.750 calculated previously

1.3e If interest compounds continuously?

Answer:

The future value of an immediate cash flow using 6.5 percent continuously compounded is

$$2 = e^{\text{Rate}_{\text{Continuous}} * \text{Years}}$$

Once again taking the natural logarithm of both sides.

$$\ln(2) = \ln(e) * \text{Rate}_{\text{Continuous}} * \text{Years}$$

$$\text{Years} = \frac{\ln(2)}{\text{Rate}_{\text{Continuous}}} = 10.664$$

1.4a What is the daily compounded rate equivalent to a semiannual 6 percent rate?

Answer:

The future value using the two rates must be equal.

$$\left(1 + \frac{\text{Rate}_{\text{semiannual}}}{2}\right)^2 = \left(1 + \frac{\text{Rate}_{\text{Daily}}}{365}\right)^{365}$$

$$1.03^2 = 1.0609 = \left(1 + \frac{\text{Rate}_{\text{Daily}}}{365}\right)^{365}$$

$$\sqrt[365]{1.0609} = 1 + \frac{\text{Rate}_{\text{Daily}}}{365}$$

$$\text{Rate}_{\text{Daily}} = 365 * \left(\sqrt[365]{1.0609} - 1\right) = 5.912\%$$

To evaluate the preceding equation using Excel, enter the following cell formula:

$$= 365 * (1.0609 \wedge (1/365) - 1)$$

In general, for any compounding period, where N is the number of compounding periods per year (for example $N_{\text{Semiannual}} = 2$),

$$\text{Equivalent Rate} = N\left(\sqrt[N]{FV}-1\right)$$

The future value factor, FV, is the future value of $1 and can be calculated from any rate, being careful to match the compounding frequency in the formula to the compounding assumed with the rate. The future value in the formula in the preceding equation is for one year in the future.

1.4b What is the monthly compounded rate equivalent to a 6 percent semiannual rate?

Answer:

$$\text{Rate}_{\text{Monthly}} = 12\left(\sqrt[12]{\left(1+\frac{6\%}{2}\right)^2} - 1\right) = 5.926\%$$

1.4c What is the annually compounded rate equivalent to a semiannual 6 percent rate?

Answer:

$$(1 + \text{Rate}_{\text{Annual}}) = \left(1 + \frac{\text{Rate}_{\text{Semiannual}}}{2}\right)^2$$

$$\text{Rate}_{\text{Annual}} = \left(1 + \frac{\text{Rate}_{\text{Semiannual}}}{2}\right)^2 - 1 = \left(1 + \frac{6\%}{2}\right)^2 - 1 = 6.090\%$$

The annually compounded rate earns interest on interest, but interest is paid on one-year intervals. The semiannually compounded rate earns more interest on interest because it receives income partway through each year. The annually compounded investment must pay a slightly higher rate to earn the same total interest as the semiannually compounded investment.

1.4d What is the continuously compounded rate equivalent to a semiannual 6 percent rate?

Answer:

$$e^{\text{Rate}_{\text{Continuous}} * \text{Years}} = \left(1 + \frac{\text{Rate}_{\text{Semiannual}}}{2}\right)^2$$

Take the log of both sides.

$$\text{Rate}_{\text{Continuous}} * 1 = 2\ln\left(1 + \frac{6\%}{2}\right)$$

$$\text{Rate}_{\text{Continuous}} = \frac{2 * 2.956\%}{1} = 5.912\%$$

As a cross check, the rates equivalent to an 6 percent annually compounded return are shown in the table that follows. The table also shows the future value calculated using each of the equivalent rates for maturities of one to four years.

Table Q.1 Check of Future Values

	Equivalent Rates					
	Continuous	Daily	Monthly	Quarterly	Semiannually	Annually
	5.827%	5.827%	5.841%	5.870%	5.913%	6.000%
Years	Continuous	Daily	Monthly	Quarterly	Semiannually	Annually
1	1.060	1.060	1.060	1.060	1.060	1.060
2	1.124	1.124	1.124	1.124	1.124	1.124
3	1.191	1.191	1.191	1.191	1.191	1.191
4	1.262	1.262	1.262	1.262	1.262	1.262

For one year:

$$1 + 6.000\% = (1 + 5.913\%/2)^2 = (1 + 5.870\%/4)^4$$
$$= (1 + 5.841\%/12)^{12} = (1 + 5.827\%/365)^{365}$$

For two years:

$$(1 + 6.000\%)^2 = (1 + 5.913\%/2)^{2*2} = (1 + 5.870\%/4)^{2*4}$$
$$= (1 + 5.841\%/12)^{2*12} = (1 + 5.827\%/365)^{2*365}$$

1.5 Following a large decline in stock prices, David commented that he lost 100 percent of the value of his 401K; then he grinned and added, "continuously compounded." If David's 401K was worth $100,000 18 months ago, what is it worth today?

Answer:

As counterintuitive as it may sound, David's account is worth $22,313. David's rate of return was −100 percent (annual rate, continuously compounded, so the future value of $100,000 over 18 months is $100,000 * e^{-100\% * 1.5}$, which equals $22,313. Of course, if David had lost 100 percent simple (no compounding), he would have nothing left in his 401K. The lognormal distribution using continuously compounded returns presented in Chapters 5 and 6 will create a distribution of prices that cannot go below 0.

CHAPTER 2

Use the following sample data to answer the questions in Chapter 2:

Return	Rank
9.70%	5
11.50%	10
8.40%	2
8.40%	3
10.90%	8
10.20%	6
9.20%	4
11.00%	9
8.30%	1
10.40%	7

2.1 What is the median return in the table of sample data?
Answer:
The median return is the return that is in the middle of the range. To determine that midpoint, it is helpful to rank the data. If there were nine data points (suppose, for example, that the largest return of 11.50 percent was not in the series), the median return would be 9.70 percent, the actual value of the data point on the top of list. Because this return is the fifth-highest of nine returns, there are four returns smaller than 9.70 percent (8.30 percent, 8.40 percent, 8.40 percent, and 9.20 percent) and four returns larger than 9.70 percent (10.20 percent, 10.40 percent, 10.90 percent, and 11.00 percent).

Because there are 10 data points, there is no single data point that represents a midpoint. Instead, two points, 9.70 percent (the fifth point) and 10.20 percent (the sixth point) determine the midpoint. The median is the midpoint or average between 9.70 percent and 10.20 percent or 9.95 percent.

2.2 What is the mean or average return of the 10 returns in the sample data?
Answer:
The average equals the sum of the 10 returns divided by 10.

The sum is

$$9.70\% + 11.50\% + 8.40\% + 8.40\% + 10.90\% + 10.20\%$$
$$+ 9.20\% + 11.00\% + 8.30\% + 10.40\% = 98.00\%$$

The average is

$$98.00\%/10 = 9.8\%$$

2.3 What is the variance of the sample data?
  Answer:
  The first column of the following table repeats the returns used previously.

Sample Data Squared Deviations

Return	Deviation	Squared Deviation
9.70%	−0.10%	0.0001%
11.50%	1.70%	0.0289%
8.40%	−1.40%	0.0196%
8.40%	−1.40%	0.0196%
10.90%	1.10%	0.0121%
10.20%	0.40%	0.0016%
9.20%	−0.60%	0.0036%
11.00%	1.20%	0.0144%
8.30%	−1.50%	0.0225%
10.40%	0.60%	0.0036%

The second column equals the difference between the returns and the mean return, 9.8 percent, calculated in Question 2.2. For example, the first return of 9.70 percent less the mean return of 9.80 percent equals −0.10 percent. Note that the deviation of −0.10 percent means that the observation is .10 less than the mean. As a practical point, it will not matter whether this middle column is calculated as the mean less the observed data point (9.8 percent − 9.70 percent = .10 percent) or the observed data point less than the mean (9.70 percent − 9.80 percent = −.10 percent).

The second return of 11.50 percent less the mean return of 9.80 percent equals 1.70 percent. The remaining values in the middle column equal the deviations of each return from the mean.

The third column labeled Squared Deviation squares the deviation. The values in this column are the squares of the deviations in the middle column. For example, the first deviation of −0.10 percent times −0.10 percent, equals 0.0001 percent. Note that the squared deviation of −.10 percent is equal to the squared deviation of .10 percent, so it wouldn't matter whether the deviation in the middle column was the observed data point less the mean or the mean less the observed data point. Similarly, the second deviation of 1.70 percent times 1.70 percent equals 0.0289 percent. The values in the third column labeled Squared Deviation equal the squares of the deviations in the middle column of the table.

The squared deviations in the right column of the table sum to 0.126 percent. The variance equals this sum divided by one less than the number of observations. The variance equals 0.126 percent/9 = 0.014 percent. The sum of squared deviations is divided by one less than the number of observations because the data consists of samples.

2.4 What is the standard deviation of the returns in the sample data?

Answer:

The standard deviation equals the positive square root of the variance calculated in Question 2.3. The square root of 0.014 percent equals 1.18 percent.

Excel functions can be used to calculate the median, mean, variance, and standard deviation. The function calls are as follows:

$$= \text{median}(9.70\%, 11.505, \dots 10.40\%)$$

The median function returns 9.95 percent.

$$= \text{average}(9.70\%, 11.505, \dots 10.40\%)$$

The average function returns 9.80 percent.

$$= \text{var}(9.70\%, 11.505, \dots 10.40\%)$$

The var function returns 0.014 percent.

$$= \text{stdev}(9.70\%, 11.505, \dots 10.40\%)$$

The stdev function returns 1.18 percent.

2.5 You are considering investing in a project. Your engineering department has reviewed many factors that could affect the profitability of the project and reports that the project has an expected profit (as measured by your accountants) of $300,000 per year. Those factors create considerable uncertainty. The engineers believe that the actual profit is normally distributed with a standard deviation of $250,000.

The CEO admits that this information is not helpful to him and asks how likely the project is to break even or lose money. Can you answer the CEO's question?

Answer:

The figure labeled Normally Distributed Expected Profit reflects the mean profit of $300,000 and standard deviation of $250,000.

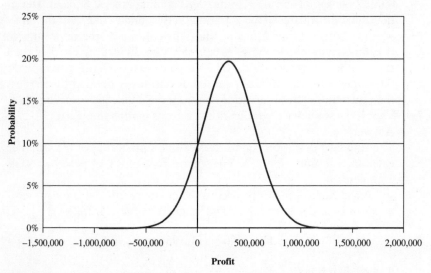

FIGURE Q.1 Normally Distributed Expected Profit

Notice that the high point on the bell chart lines up with a profit of $300,000. Because the curve is symmetrical, an outcome of $250,000 ($50,000 lower than $300,000) is exactly as likely as an outcome of $350,000 ($50,000 higher than $300,000). Similarly, an outcome of $200,000 ($100,000 lower than $300,000) is exactly as likely as an outcome of $400,000 ($100,000 higher than $300,000). This equally offsetting pattern holds for any profit potential. As a result, the average of these outcomes must be $300,000.

The probability of each outcome appears in the figure labeled Normally Distributed Expected Profit. The probability of losing money equals the part of the curve below $0. This probability appears visually in the figure as the area below the curve and to the left of the line. The probability of each level of profitability of the project completes the distribution shown in the figure.

From the cumulative profit chart in the figure labeled Cumulative Distribution of Expected Profit, you can observe the probability of net

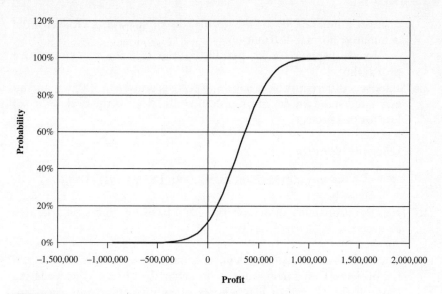

FIGURE Q.2   Cumulative Distribution of Expected Profit

income below zero. It appears that the net income is at break-even or a loss about 11 or 12 percent of the time.

Statistics textbooks generally provide a table of probabilities on the normal distribution. Excel provides a way to precisely determine the probability that the income will be $0 or less. The probability distribution in Q.2 is called the cumulative normal density (or probability) function. To use Excel's function, type

$$= \text{NormDist}(0, \text{Mean}, \text{Standard Deviation}, \text{TRUE})$$

$$= \text{NormDist}(0, 300000, 250000, \text{TRUE})$$

The value 0 instructs Excel to return the probability of a loss. In statistical terms, this is the value of the left tail starting at zero.

The NormDist function also needs to know the mean and standard deviation of the distribution. This is the mathematical equivalent of informing the function how to draw the Cumulative Probability of Profit.

Finally, the NormDist function can calculate the normal probability (the probability of observing a particular value) or the cumulative normal probability or the probability of observing a particular value or less). Enter FALSE for the normal distribution and TRUE for the cumulative normal distribution.

Excel displays 11.51 percent in the cell for the cumulative probability.

2.6 Suppose a different project has an expected return of $500,000 and an estimated standard deviation of $500,000. What is the probability of loss for this project?

Answer:

Using the NormDist function:

$$= Normdist(0, 500000, 500000, TRUE) = 15.87\%$$

2.7 Does the probability of default provide a basis for comparing the two projects?

Answer:

The break-even probability is not a commonly used basis for comparing projects. Companies want to do better than break even. Focusing only on the chance of loss ignores other important outcomes. For example, it may be more important that the second project has a higher expected profit.

Furthermore, the standard deviation may not be an adequate measure of risk. As described in Chapter 2, investors can achieve substantial risk reduction through diversification. The standard deviation can be a useful input if the correlation or covariance is known.

2.8 Suppose that the company can invest an equal amount in both of the projects in Questions 2.5–2.6. Further, the correlation of returns is .40. What is the mean net income and the standard deviation?

Answer:

It might be possible to invest half of the intended amount in each of the projects. In that case, the weights of the two projects (w_A and w_B) both equal .50. The weights sum to 1, or 100 percent of the original budget. Suppose, instead, that you can invest in both projects and double your capital budget. In this case, the weights would each equal 1 and would sum to 2, or 200 percent of the original budget. Nevertheless, Equations 2.11 to 2.13 can measure the risk and return of the combined investment.

Equation 2.11 in the text describes the return on two projects. The same equation can be used to combine the uncertain profits of the two projects. The mean of the sum of the two projects equals the sum of the means of the individual projects. Therefore, the expected profit is $300,000 + $500,000 or $800,000.

$$\text{Profit}_{\text{Portfolio}} = \text{Profit}_A * w_A + \text{Profit}_B * w_B$$

$$\text{Profit}_{\text{Portfolio}} = \$300,000 * 1 + \$500,000 * 1 = \$800,000$$

The formula confirms what may already be clear to the reader, that investing in both projects produces expected profits that equal the total of expected profits of each individual project.

The standard deviation of the portfolio that includes both projects benefits from the diversification of outcomes. The correlation of the possible outcomes is .40, so many times good results from one project offset weak results from the other project.

The standard deviation for a portfolio was presented in the text in Equation 2.12. That equation requires the covariance between the two projects. The covariance was described in Equation 2.10.

$$\text{Covariance}_{A,B} = \text{Correlation}_{A,B} * \text{Standard deviation}_A * \text{Standard deviation}_B$$

Using the correlation of .40, the standard deviation of the first project equal to \$250,000, and the standard deviation of the second project,

$$\text{Covariance}_{A,B} = .40 * 250,000 * 500,000 = 50,000,000,000$$

Next, applying the formula (based on Equation 2.12),

$$\sigma_{\text{Portfolio}} = \sqrt{w_A^2 \sigma_A^2 + 2 w_A w_B \sigma_{A,B} + w_B^2 \sigma_B^2}$$

Inserting the values from the previous questions,

$$\sigma_{\text{Portfolio}} = \sqrt{1^2 * 250,000^2 + 2 * 1 * 1 * 50 \text{ billion} + 1^2 * 500,000^2}$$

Next, evaluate the three terms,

$$\sigma_{\text{Portfolio}} = \sqrt{62.5 \text{ billion} + 100 \text{ billion} + 250 \text{ billion}} = 642,262$$

This measure of risk is well below the sum of the two individual standard deviations (\$250,000 + \$500,000 equals \$750,000). The standard deviation reflects the correlation of .40, so that a portfolio of two projects diversifies away part of the risk of individual projects.

The table that follows displays the standard deviation of the two projects at different correlation assumptions, including 0 (uncorrelated) and 1.00 (perfect correlation) using the above equation. If the outcome of the two projects is perfectly correlated, there is no diversification benefit. The standard deviation of the combined investment equals the sum of the standard deviation of the individual projects or $750,000. If the projects are uncorrelated, the standard deviation of the combination is lower ($559,017). In fact, even if the profits from the two projects are perfectly negatively correlated, the returns on one project hedge the returns of the second project. However, the lower standard deviation of Project A cannot hedge all of the uncertainty of the return on Project B.

Impact of Correlation on Combined Standard Deviation

Correlation	Standard Deviation
−1.00	250,000
−0.75	353,553
−0.50	433,013
−0.25	500,000
0.00	559,017
0.25	612,372
0.50	661,438
0.75	707,107
1.00	750,000

2.9 Suppose that you can invest in a number of projects and the return on each of the projects is completely uncorrelated. What can you say about the standard deviation of the portfolio?
Answer:
Diversification with several assets can reduce the standard deviation below the risk of the individual assets. In fact, because the returns on the individual projects are uncorrelated, you can diversify away much of the risk.

A portfolio of a very large number of uncorrelated returns resembles the business of some insurance products and a gambling casino. Unless some individual exposures are large (e.g., a very high roller betting with no house limits), the low correlation of the outcomes permits the company to diversify away virtually all of the uncertainty of outcomes.

2.10 Use the data that follows to calculate the beta for IBM versus the S&P 500. Ignore dividends and assume that the risk-free rate is 5 percent.
Answer:
The important first step is to calculate excess returns for the S&P 500 and IBM. As suggested previously, the return should include dividends received. Both the size and timing of dividends affect the returns.

Closing Prices for S&P 500 and IBM

Date	S&P 500	IBM
12/29/2006	1,418.30	93.16
1/31/2007	1,438.24	95.08
2/28/2007	1,406.82	89.39
3/30/2007	1,420.86	90.66
4/30/2007	1,482.37	98.31
5/31/2007	1,530.62	102.93
6/29/2007	1,503.35	101.62
7/31/2007	1,455.27	106.84
8/31/2007	1,473.99	113.07
9/28/2007	1,526.75	114.14
10/31/2007	1,549.38	112.52
11/30/2007	1,481.14	102.28
12/31/2007	1,468.36	105.12

However, the dividends on the S&P 500 are paid on various dates, which require some kind of adjustment for the timing. For simplicity, we ignore dividends.

The table that follows shows the monthly return on both the S&P 500 and IBM less 5 percent/12. These are simple returns (ending price divided by beginning price less 1) and are not adjusted for the slightly different dates in the months.

Excess Return for S&P 500 and IBM

Date	S&P 500	IBM
12/29/2006	n.a.	n.a.
1/31/2007	0.99%	1.64%
2/28/2007	−2.60%	−6.40%
3/30/2007	0.58%	1.00%
4/30/2007	3.91%	8.02%
5/31/2007	2.84%	4.28%
6/29/2007	−2.20%	−1.69%
7/31/2007	−3.61%	4.72%
8/31/2007	0.87%	5.41%
9/28/2007	3.16%	0.53%
10/31/2007	1.07%	−1.84%
11/30/2007	−4.82%	−9.52%
12/31/2007	−1.28%	2.36%

The covariance of IBM to the S&P 500 is .000809. The variance of the S&P 500 is .000717 using Equation 2.5a. Therefore, the beta of IBM relative to the S&P is .000809/.000717 = 1.129. (This beta is calculated from the population statistics but the sample statistics provide the same beta.)

As a cross check, a regression of IBM returns versus the S&P 500 produces a slope or beta of 1.129. The dependent or Y variable is the excess return on IBM. The independent or X variable is the excess return on the S&P 500.

One way to run the regression in Excel is to use the formula

$$= \text{slope}(Y : Y, X : X)$$

where Y:Y refers to the cells on the worksheet containing IBM returns from the foregoing table and X:X refers to the cells containing S&P 500 returns.

2.11 What is the alpha of IBM using the foregoing prices for IBM and the S&P 500 for 2007?

Answer:
The regression of IBM versus the S&P 500 produces both a slope (beta) and an intercept (alpha). One way to recover the intercept in Excel is to use the formula

$$= \text{intercept}(Y : Y, X : X)$$

The formula returns .81 percent.

The regression intercept shows the alpha for IBM. The beta describes how IBM returns adjust on a somewhat leveraged basis to S&P 500 returns. However, the returns are .81 percent higher than the return "explained" by S&P market returns and beta. The line is .81 percent higher at all points, but it is easiest to see the alpha at the point where S&P 500 excess returns are 0 percent, because IBM fitted return is .81 percent above 0 percent.

This regression means that, over the year, IBM returns tended to move up and down a little more than the S&P from month to month.

The CAPM equation is:

$$r_{\text{IBM}} - r_{\text{Risk-free}} = 1.129 * (r_{\text{S&P}} - r_{\text{Risk-free}}) + .81\%$$

CHAPTER 3

3.1 Your company can issue new debt at 8.15 percent (including all issuing costs and fees). The company's marginal tax rate is 35 percent. What is the after-tax cost of debt capital for the company?

Answer:

The cost of debt financing net of the tax savings is 8.15 percent ∗ (1 − 35 percent) or 5.30 percent.

3.2 Your company has a pretax cost of debt of 8.15 percent, an equity cost of capital of 12 percent, and a corporate tax rate of 35 percent. The company's debt-to-equity ratio is .6, and it plans to maintain that ratio. What is the firm's weighted average cost of capital (WACC)?

Answer:

The formula for WACC relies on the ratio of debt to total capital and the ratio of equity to total capital. The debt-to-equity ratio measures the total value of debt to the total value of equity. The problem does not provide the actual amounts of debt, but the ratio documents the relative amounts of debt and equity on the firm's balance sheet.

For each dollar of equity, the company has $.60 of debt. On these reduced amounts, there is $.60 of debt to $1.60 of total capital ($.60 debt plus $1 equity) or 37.5 percent. There is $1 of equity to 1.60 of total capital or 62.5 percent.

$$\text{WACC} = 62.5\% * 12\% + 37.5\% * (1 - 35\%) * 8.15\% = 9.49\%$$

3.3 Using the information in Question 3.2, what is the company's average return on assets?

Answer:

The return on assets goes either to the debt holders or the equity share holders. The weighted average return on assets (the return on the accounts on the left or debit side of the balance sheet) must match the return on the accounts on the right or credit side of the balance sheet. This average closely resembles the WACC except that the WACC uses the after-tax cost of debt.

$$\text{Average Return on Assets} = 62.5\% * 12\% + 37.5\% * 8.15\% = 10.56\%$$

CHAPTER 4

4.1 Suppose your current income would permit you to make a $2,000 per month mortgage payment. What is the maximum loan you can get if mortgage rates are 5 percent for a 15-year loan? What loan amount could you borrow at 5.5 percent on a 30-year loan?

Answer:

$$PV = PMT * \frac{1 - \dfrac{1}{(1 + \text{Rate}/12)^{N*12}}}{\text{Rate}/12}$$

Rate N (months)
5.00% 15 * 12
5.50% 30 * 12
For a 15-year loan:

$$PV = 2,000 * \frac{1 - \dfrac{1}{(1 + 5\%/12)^{180}}}{5\%/12} = \$252,910$$

For a 30-year loan:

$$PV = 2,000 * \frac{1 - \dfrac{1}{(1 + 5.5\%/12)^{360}}}{5.5\%/12} = 352,244$$

The annuity formula produces exactly the same value as arrived at through valuation summing the present value of 180 and 360 cash flows.

Value of Mortgage Payments

Month	Cash Flow	PV@5%	Cash Flow	PV@5.5%
1	2,000	1,991.70	2,000	1,990.88
2	2,000	1,983.44	2,000	1,981.79
3	2,000	1,975.21	2,000	1,972.75
. . . . . .	. . . . . .	. . . . . .	. . . . . .	. . . . . .
179	2,000	950.15	2,000	882.15
180	2,000	946.21	2,000	878.12
181	0	0.00	2,000	874.12
. . . . . .	. . . . . .	. . . . . .	. . . . . .	. . . . . .
359	0	0.00	2,000	387.32
360	0	0.00	2,000	385.55
		252,910		352,244

The 15-year cash flows are discounted at 5 percent. These cash flows continue for 180 months. The 30-year cash flows are discounted at 5.5

percent. These cash flows continue for 360 months. The table displays only the first three months, months 179–181, and months 359–360, but the totals at the bottom include all the hidden months.

Using the annuity formula in Excel requires careful attention to the order in which calculations are performed. For example, the addition of the interest rate to 1 must be performed before the sum is raised to a power. Both of these operations must be complete before the result is divided into one. Use parentheses to ensure that Excel performs the operations in the proper order.

To value the 15-year mortgage at 5 percent, use the following formula:

$$= 2000 * (1 - (1/(1 + 5\%/12)\wedge(15 * 12)))/(5\%/12)$$

Excel has a function that will calculate the value of an annuity. The formula returns the same answers as the annuity formula in Equation 4.9; it is easier to use and less prone to errors in translating the formula into a value. To value the 15-year mortgage with a 5 percent interest rate, use the following formula:

$$= PV(5\%/12, 15 * 12, -2000)$$

More generally, pass the interest rate, the number of periods, and the cash flows to the PV function. The interest rate should be deannualized. Divide the annual rate by the number of periods per year. The preceding equation divides the 5 percent annual-monthly compounded rate by 12. Similarly, divide a quarterly-compounded rate by 4 and a semiannual rate by 2.

The second input is the number of periods during which the cash flow will occur. Because the 15-year mortgage requires monthly payments, there are 15 * 12 or 180 payments. The 30-year mortgage requires 30 * 12 or 360 payments.

The PV function returns the present value of positive cash flows as a negative number and the present value of negative numbers as a positive. The convention of the PV function makes sense if the annuity is viewed as an investment. An investment or loan made by a bank would require a cash outflow of $252,912 and would receive monthly inflows of $2,000. Similarly, the borrower receives $252,912 (a cash inflow), which is used to buy a house, and then must make monthly payments (cash outflows) of $2,000. The Excel annuity formula reflects the point of view of the borrower, who has cash outflows (negative payments) and a receipt of cash at the time the loan is created.

4.2 Camilla needs to borrow $400,000. Mortgage rates are at 6 percent for both a 15-year and a 30-year loan. How much could she reduce her monthly cash payment by picking the loan with the lower payment?
Answer:
The payment of an annuity can be derived from the annuity formula presented in Equation 4.9 in the text. The simplified formula for the payment is:

$$Pmt = Principal/((1 - (1/(1 + Rate/12) \wedge No. \text{ of Months}))/(Rate/12))$$

Applying the equation for a 15-year mortgage (180 months):

$$Pmt = 400000/((1 - (1/(1 + 6\%/12) \wedge 180))/(6\%/12)) = \$3,375$$

Applying the equation for 30-year mortgage (360 months):

$$Pmt = 400000/((1 - (1/(1 + 6\%/12) \wedge 360))/(6\%/12)) = \$2,398$$

The 15-year mortgage payment is $977 less than the 30-year mortgage.
    Note that Excel has a function (PMT) that will determine the payment on an ordinary annuity.

$$Payment = PMT(Rate/12, Months, Principal)$$

Applying the function for the 15 year mortgage:

$$= PMT(6\%/12, 180, -400,000)$$

Table Q.2 Cash Flows of Two Projects

	Project 1	Project 2
Year	Cash Flow	Cash Flow
0	($10,000,000)	($10,000,000)
1	3,000,000	1,700,000
2	3,000,000	1,700,000
3	3,000,000	1,700,000
4	3,000,000	1,700,000
5	0	1,700,000
6	0	1,700,000
7	0	1,700,000
8	0	1,700,000
9	0	1,700,000
10	0	1,700,000

The function returns the value of $3,375.

Applying the function for the 30-year mortgage:

$$= PMT(6\%/12, 360, -400,000)$$

The function returns the value of $2,398.

Use the following assumptions for the two projects under review.

4.3a Calculate the payback period for each of these two projects.

Answer:

Each of the projects would require an investment of $10 million immediately. Project 1 would receive $3 million each year continuing for four years, and Project 2 would produce $1.7 million each year continuing for 10 years. Neither project would have any salvage value, and neither project would have termination costs at the end of its useful life.

Table Q.3 Payback of Two Projects

	Project 1		Project 2	
Year	Cash Flow	Net Cash Flow	Cash Flow	Net Cash Flow
0	($10,000,000)	($10,000,000)	($10,000,000)	($10,000,000)
1	3,000,000	(7,000,000)	1,700,000	(8,300,000)
2	3,000,000	(4,000,000)	1,700,000	(6,600,000)
3	3,000,000	(1,000,000)	1,700,000	(4,900,000)
4	3,000,000	2,000,000	1,700,000	(3,200,000)
5	0	2,000,000	1,700,000	(1,500,000)
6	0	2,000,000	1,700,000	200,000
7	0	2,000,000	1,700,000	1,900,000
8	0	2,000,000	1,700,000	3,600,000
9	0	2,000,000	1,700,000	5,300,000
10	0	2,000,000	1,700,000	7,000,000

Table Q.3 displays the net cash flows of Project 1 and Project 2. The net cash flow is initially equal to the $10 million initial investment. As each project generates annual cash flows, the net cash outflow is reduced by the annual receipt. Project 1 has a net cash flow equal to ($1 million) at the end of the third year and is positive after the fourth year. Project 2 has a net cash flow equal to ($1.5 million) at the end of the fifth year and a positive net cash flow after the sixth year.

In each case, this solution assumes that the cash flows for both projects are received at the end of each year. If the cash is received steadily throughout the year, Project 1 would have received $10 million of cash inflows by one-third of the way through the fourth year, so it could be realistic to conclude that the payback is 3.33 years. Similarly if the cash is received steadily throughout the year, Project 2 would have received $10 million in cash inflows a little before the end of the sixth year. 1,500,000/1,700,000 = .88. Project 2 returns $10 million in 5.88 years.

4.3b Based solely on the payback period, which investment appears to be more attractive?

Answer:

Based on the payback model, Project 1 appears to be more attractive, because it has a shorter payback period. However, the cash flows stop on Project 1 just after the payback period whereas the cash flows continue for four years after reaching the payback period for Project 2. The payback model ignores the cash flows occurring after the payback date; consequently, it does not consider the impact of these cash flows on the investment decision.

4.4a Assume that the cost of capital for the company considering the projects previously mentioned is 14 percent compounded annually. What is the net present value of each project whose cash flows are listed in Table Q.2?

Table Q.4 NPV of Two Projects

	Project 1		Project 2	
Year	Cash Flow	Present Value	Cash Flow	Present Value
0	($10,000,000)	($10,000,000)	($10,000,000)	($10,000,000)
1	3,000,000	2,631,579	1,700,000	1,491,228
2	3,000,000	2,308,403	1,700,000	1,308,095
3	3,000,000	2,024,915	1,700,000	1,147,452
4	3,000,000	1,776,241	1,700,000	1,006,536
5	0	0	1,700,000	882,927
6	0	0	1,700,000	774,497
7	0	0	1,700,000	679,383
8	0	0	1,700,000	595,950
9	0	0	1,700,000	522,764
10	0	0	1,700,000	458,564
	NPV	−1,258,863	NPV	−1,132,603

Answer:
Table Q.4 reproduces the cash flows from Table Q.2 but now includes the present value of each cash flow and the sum of the present value of the individual cash flows.

4.4b Based solely on the net present value of Project 1 and Project 2, which investment appears to be more attractive?

Answer:
The net present value of both projects is negative. Neither project earns a high enough return if the required return is 14 percent. Still, a company may be required to invest in some projects. For example, a company may need to invest in equipment to comply with pollution regulations or to invest in one of these projects even if the NPV is negative, because the company must complete one of the projects to be able to make other highly profitable investments.

If the company must invest in either Project 1 or Project 2, it should invest in Project 2 because it has a higher NPV.

Note that the internal rate of return on Project 1 is 7.71 percent and the internal rate of return on Project 2 is 11.03 percent. Based on the internal rate of return on each project, Project 2 is also the better project for the company.

4.5 Your company issued debt two years ago with an 8 percent semiannual coupon. The issue now has five years remaining until maturity. The fair market price of the debt is 104.25 (per $100 face amount). What is the pretax cost of debt for the company?

Answer:
The current cost of debt is approximately equal to the yield on the outstanding issue. The yield on the existing bond is equal to the internal rate of return of the cash flows based on the current market price. The 8 percent coupon is not a measure of the company's current cost of debt.

The table that follows sets out the cash flows for the bond. Each cash flow is discounted to the present. The internal rate of return is the yield that sets the value of the future cash payments equal to the current market price. Or, using the capital budgeting language, the price of 104.25 is the investment (a cash outflow). The yield is the rate that makes the value of all cash flows (the initial outflow of 104.25, the semiannual inflows, and the maturity) equal to zero.

To determine the IRR, choose a discount rate and vary the rate until the NPV equals zero. For the company's bond, this yield is 6.978502 percent.

Note that the annuity formula provides a convenient way to value the bond without constructing a table of each cash flow and can be

Internal Rate of Return (Yield) on 5-Year Bond

Year	Cash Flow	Present Value
0.00	($104.25)	($104.250)
0.50	4.00	3.865
1.00	4.00	3.735
1.50	4.00	3.609
2.00	4.00	3.487
2.50	4.00	3.370
3.00	4.00	3.256
3.50	4.00	3.146
4.00	4.00	3.040
4.50	4.00	2.938
5.00	104.00	73.804
NPV		0.000

used to cross check the preceding results. The Excel formula PV values the semiannual payments.

$$= PV(\text{Yield, Number of Payments, Size of Payment})$$

$$= PV(6.978502\%/2, 10, -4) = 33.284$$

The value of the maturity payment is

$$= 100/(1 + 6.978502\%/2)^{\wedge}(2 * 5) = 70.966$$

The value of the bond is $33.284 + 70.966 = 104.25$. Alternatively, the NPV of the cash flows is $-104.25 + 33.284 + 70.966$.

Of course, the annuity formula could be used instead of the table to search for the yield (or IRR). To use the annuity formula and the value of the principal, start with a guess for the yield and decide whether the value of the coupons and principal equals 104.25 (and the NPV equals zero). Adjust the yield until the value of the cash flows matches the bond price.

If the company has more than one debt issue outstanding or if the company would pay a significantly higher or lower yield on bonds issued for maturities other than five years, it may want to consider that additional information. The company might also want to adjust the yield to include the underwriting costs it would incur to issue more debt.

4.6 Suppose the 8 percent bond described in Question 4.5 matured in exactly 4.75 years. The market price is still 104.25. What is the company's pretax cost of debt capital?

Answer:

The table of cash flows is similar to the table immediately preceding. The bond will still make 10 semiannual payments. Each cash flow will be .25 years closer, so the payments are discounted by a different amount. In addition, the buyer of the bond had to pay no accrued interest in Question 4.5 because the pricing occurred on a coupon payment date. Now, the pricing occurs halfway through the semiannual period. The buyer pays the seller $2 of accrued interest (half of the $4 semiannual coupon).

Internal Rate of Return (Yield) on a 4.75-Year Bond

Year	Cash Flow	Present Value
0.00	($106.25)	($106.250)
0.25	4.00	3.932
0.75	4.00	3.801
1.25	4.00	3.673
1.75	4.00	3.550
2.25	4.00	3.432
2.75	4.00	3.317
3.25	4.00	3.206
3.75	4.00	3.098
4.25	4.00	2.994
4.75	104.00	75.247
NPV		0.000

The previous yield does not match the value of the cash flows to the bond price anymore. By trial and error, the values match using a yield of 6.93038 percent. The pretax cost of debt capital is 6.93 percent.

The Excel function YIELD calculates this answer and is simpler to use than either a table of cash flows or the annuity function (PV). An example of the YIELD function is as follows:

> = YIELD(Settle, Maturity, Coupon, Price, Redemptions, Compounding, DayCount)

The following inputs could be used to determine the yield on a 4.75-year bond:

$$= \text{YIELD}(\text{``}8/15/09,\text{''} \text{``}5/15/14,\text{''} \ 8\%, 104.25, 100, 2, 1) = 6.930\%$$

(Note that a compounding code of 2 means semiannual and a day-counting code of 1 uses actual day counting. For more information on day counting, see the appendix).

The YIELD function also finds the yield by trial and error but the function conducts the search for the user.

CHAPTER 5

5.1 Your city is voting on a bond issue that the local newspaper has predicted has a 75 percent chance of passing. If the referendum passes, your company has a 65 percent chance of winning the job of general contractor, a 30 percent chance of handling only the site preparation, and a 5 percent chance of getting no work. If the referendum fails, there is a 60 percent chance you will win the job of general contractor of a smaller stadium renovation project and a 40 percent chance of getting no work. Construct a tree to determine the probability of each scenario.

Answer:

The tree shown in Figure Q.3 describes the range of possible outcomes. The tree converts three sources of uncertainty into five scenarios or outcomes.

The five scenarios and the probability of each are listed in the table that follows:

Probability of Scenarios on Bond Issue Tree

Scenario	Formula	Probability	Description
1	75% * 65%	48.75%	General Contractor
2	75% * 30%	22.50%	Site Preparation
3	75% * 5%	3.75%	No Work
4	25% * 60%	15.00%	General Contractor
5	25% * 40%	10.00%	No Work

One of the scenarios appears twice on the table. The scenarios reduce to:

Simplified Probability of Scenarios on Bond Issue Tree

Scenario	Formula	Probability
General Contractor Major	48.75%	48.75%
Site Preparation	22.50%	22.50%
General Contractor Renovation	15.00%	15.00%
No Work	3.75% + 10.00%	13.75%

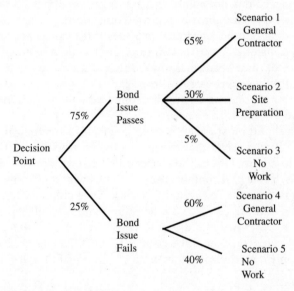

FIGURE Q.3   Stadium Proposal Tree

5.2 Use Monte Carlo simulation to estimate the chance of flipping a coin three times and coming up with heads three times?

Answer:

This problem has an exact solution and might be a good problem for a statistics textbook. We know that there is a 50 percent chance of flipping a real head on the first toss. Then, if that happens, there is a 50 percent chance of flipping a second head (50 percent * 50 percent = 25 percent). If the toss comes up twice, there is a 50 percent chance of getting a third (25 percent * 50 percent = 12.5 percent). Monte Carlo can also solve the problem, and it provides a good introduction to random number generators.

The first task is to create outcomes. Excel and many programming languages have random number generators that return a value between

0 and 1. Unlike the normal distribution, the outcomes near 0 and 1 are each as likely as outcomes near the mean. A simple rule can simulate a coin toss. For example, the model could assume that a value of .50 or less is a head and a value greater than .50 is a tail. As an aside, it wouldn't matter if values greater than .50 were considered heads and the lower values were tails. It also should not matter much whether the value of exactly .50 is a head or a tail, because that value is only one outcome among the millions of decimal values between 0 and 1 that a well-designed random number generator can produce.

The experience must be repeated three times for each trial. That is, the random number generator provides three values and the result of the experiment is either that all three are less than or equal to .50 (occurrence of three heads in a row) or that at least one value was greater than .50 (nonoccurrence of three heads in a row). The experiment is then repeated many times to determine how often the random draws result in three heads in a row.

Excel and most programming languages have logical statements such as IF and AND that can be combined to detect a trial of three heads in a row. Often, the test can use mathematics to simplify the analysis. Table Q.5 contains three columns with uniformly distributed random numbers. To the right of these three columns are three more columns that are equal to 1 when the random number is equal to or less than .50 (a head) and 0 otherwise. Finally, a column on the right multiplies together the three values of 1 or 0. The result is a value of 1 if and only if all three random numbers are equal to or less than .50.

Table Q.5 Probability of Three Heads on Coin Flip

Trial	U1	U2	U3	Coin1	Coin2	Coin3	Success
1	0.112	0.414	0.959	1	1	0	0
2	0.128	0.204	0.186	1	1	1	1
.	.	.	.	.	.	.	.
.	.	.	.	.	.	.	.
.	.	.	.	.	.	.	.
99	0.855	0.655	0.135	0	0	1	0
100	0.985	0.576	0.048	0	0	1	0
Average	0.490	0.516	0.457	49%	46%	58%	11%

The results in the table come from an actual simulation. The result of 100 trials does not produce an accurate estimate of the true probability. When the same experiment was repeated with different random numbers, the results were sometimes above the expected result of 12.5 percent and sometimes below the expected result. Monte Carlo can provide accurate information about probabilities and potential outcomes only if the experiment accurately recreates a physical coin toss and if enough trials are conducted to assure accurate results.

5.3 You predict sales of 200,000 units next year. You believe that the actual sales volume is normally distributed with a standard deviation of 50,000. You have a fixed cost of $2 million and a gross margin of $15 per unit. Use Monte Carlo to determine the expected gross profit. What is the chance of losing money next year?

Answer:

Table Q.6 displays the gross profit for several samples of unit sales. The gross profit equals $15 per unit times the sampled sales less the fixed cost of $2 million.

Table Q.6 Distribution of Profitability

Trial	Uniform	Normal	Unit Sales	Gross Profit
1	0.549	0.122	206,096	1,091,440
2	0.103	−1.266	136,678	50,170
.	.	.	.	
.	.	.	.	
.	.	.	.	
999	0.341	−0.411	179,465	691,975
1000	0.312	−0.491	175,453	631,795
Average	0.500	0.007	200,352	1,005,283
Standard deviation	0.287	0.998	49,908	748,616
Maximum	0.999	3.104	355,224	3,328,360
Minimum	0.000	−3.871	6,432	1,903,520
			Number of Losses	93
		Percent of samples experiencing loss		9.30%
		Probability of loss using average and standard deviation		8.97%

Table Q.6 lists part of 1,000 samples of unit sales. Additional trials of other numbers produce generally consistent results, suggesting that the sample size is adequate. Several key statistics provide significant information about the possible profitability of the business. In addition to the mean, the standard deviation, the minimum, and the maximum, the samples provide information about the chance of loss. The samples produce 93 instances of losses, or 9.30 percent of the 1,000 trials. In addition, the cumulative distribution provides a second estimate of the probability of loss, using the mean and standard deviation of the samples.

To use Excel's NORMDIST function to calculate the probability of loss, input the average and standard deviation from the trials above:

$$= \text{NORMDIST}(0, 1005283, 748616, \text{TRUE})$$

which returns 8.97 percent.

5.4 You forecast sales equal to 100,000 units. You think there is a 25 percent chance that sales will be as low as 75,000. The sales price is also uncertain. You predict a sales price of $10 per unit but you believe that there is a 35 percent chance that the price will be below 8. Fixed cost is $500,000 and variable costs are $4 per unit. Calculate the mean and standard deviation of gross profit.

Answer:

Determining the inputs for simulations is often the hardest part of the analysis. In this case, the firm starts with a clear idea of the most likely scenario but no clear idea of what standard deviation fairly represents the uncertainty necessary to obtain a meaningful range of outcomes and whether it is reasonable to use the normal distribution. In this case, the manager has an idea about the likelihood of an outcome that is different from the one proposed in the most likely scenario.

The first task is to determine the standard deviation. The cumulative probability of observing sales 75,000 or less is 25 percent. With a mean of 100,000, the standard deviation must be 37,065. One way to find this standard deviation is to use the NORMDIST function in Excel and then search for the standard deviation that returns the right cumulative probability. Set up the function:

$$= \text{NORMDIST}(75000, 100000, 37065, \text{TRUE})$$

then try different values for the third input (the standard deviation) until the function returns 25 percent. The GOAL SEEK utility can assist this search.

Or use the inverse of the normal distribution to find out how extreme the unit sales is relative to the normal distribution. The probability of observing a standard normal value called z 25 percent of the time requires a z value of $-.674$. To calculate this z in Excel, use the NORMSINV function or look up the value shown in standard tables in a statistics book.

$$z = \text{Normsinv}(\text{Probability}) = \text{Normsinv}(25\%) = -.674$$

To convert the mean of 100,000 and the 75,000 to a standard normal *z* value, use the following adjustment:

$$z = \frac{X - \overline{X}}{\sigma}$$

Next, input the known values.

$$-.674 = \frac{75,000 - 100,000}{\sigma}$$

Finally, solve for the standard deviation.

$$\sigma = \frac{75,000 - 100,000}{-.674} = 37,065$$

Similarly, the cumulative probability of observing a sales price below $8 is 35 percent. With a mean of $10, the standard deviation must be $5.16.

$$z = \text{Normsinv(Probability)} = \text{Normsinv}(35\%) = -.38532$$

To convert the mean of 10 and the 8 to a standard normal *z* value, use the following adjustment:

Input the known values.

$$-.38532 = \frac{8 - 10}{\sigma}$$

Finally, solve for the standard deviation.

$$\sigma = \frac{8 - 10}{-.38532} = 5.19$$

A simulation following the general procedure above produced gross profit that averaged about $100,000 with a standard deviation of about $600,000.

5.5 A call gives the owner the right to buy raw materials at $100 per ton one year from now. You can buy the material now at $100 per ton, but you prefer to buy an option. Use Monte Carlo analysis to value the call assuming a 5 percent interest rate (continuously compounded) and a volatility of 15 percent (volatility is the standard deviation used for a lognormal distribution).

Answer:
The first step is to find the adjusted forward price as a starting point. Filling in the known information for Equation 5.7 from Chapter 5,

$$\text{Starting Price} = 100 * e^{(5\% - 0)*1 - \frac{15\%^2}{2*1}}$$

The starting price is 103.951.

The next step is to draw normally distributed random returns and create sample ending prices. The ending price equals the starting price (103.951) times the constant e raised to the power equal to the random return (i.e., e^{rt}, but t has a value of 1 so it does not affect this calculation). Four returns from a particular Monte Carlo experiment appear below. The trials produce an average price of 105.240, close to the expected forward price of 105.127 (i.e., 100 times e raised to the power of 5 percent). By repeating the trials with other sets of 1,000 numbers, it appears that the starting price of 103.951 does produce a set of prices whose average is equal to the forward price.

The third step is to determine the ending value of the call for each ending commodity price. If the ending price is greater than 100, the ending value (usually called the "intrinsic value") of the call equals the ending price minus 100. If the ending price of the commodity is less than or equal to 100, the intrinsic value of the call equals 0, because it is possible to buy the raw materials at the same or lower price. For example, the final sampled return produces a price of 80.786. The right to buy at 100 is worthless if it is possible to buy the commodity cheaper.

Finally, the value of the call equals the average of all the call intrinsic values discounted at 5 percent. The average of the call intrinsic values is 9.130. The present value of this average is 8.684.

Table Q.7 Valuing a Call by Monte Carlo Simulation

Trial	Normal	Lognormal	Price	Call Value
1	0.965	14.479%	120.146	20.146
2	0.104	1.560%	105.585	5.585
.	.	.	.	.
.	.	.	.	.
.	.	.	.	.
999	1.561	23.409%	131.369	31.369
1000	−1.681	−25.211%	80.786	0.000
Average	0.009	0.141%	105.240	9.130
			Call	8.684

5.6 Create a new version of Table 5.6 from Chapter 5 in which the correlation between price and unit sales is .50.

Answer:

The problem requires correlated random numbers so that a lower sales price is correlated with a lower unit sales volume and a higher sales price is correlated with a higher sales volume. This pattern may occur when the overall strength of the economy affects not only the ability to sell more goods but also the price at which they can be sold.

Annual Budget with Correlated Price and Unit Sales

Trial	Norm1	Norm2	Sales Price	Quantity	Gross Profit
1	0.018	0.142	100.14	1,012,446	20,640,503
2	0.045	−0.562	100.36	957,743	18,657,976
3	1.252	0.926	110.01	1,149,172	37,472,722
.	.	.	.	.	.
.	.	.	.	.	.
.	.	.	.	.	.
1,000	−2.160	0.458	82.72	907,003	604,057
Average	0.018	0.004	100.14	1,001,438	20,675,327
Standard deviation	0.994	0.987	7.95	98,923	10,769,185

The columns labeled Norm1 and Norm2 are standard normal random numbers (mean of zero and standard deviation of 1). The sales price was created from Norm1 by multiplying Norm1 by 8 (the standard deviation of price assumed in the original example) and adding 100 (the average price assumed in the original example). The column labeled Quantity blends together the random numbers from Norm1 and Norm2. The procedure first creates a new standard normal series (Norm1 * correlation plus Norm2 * the square root of 1 minus correlation squared). Then multiply this combined standard normal series by the standard deviation of unit sales (100,000) and add the average (1,000,000). The sales price in this particular trial has a correlation of .603 to the sampled unit sales.

Revenues and expenses are calculated the same way as the example in Chapter 5 although they are not displayed here. Revenues equal the sales price times the unit sales. Expenses equal $20 million fixed cost plus $60 times the sampled unit volume. The net income equals revenues less expenses.

As the results demonstrate, this experiment appears to have similar inputs. The price in both trials averages near $100, with a standard deviation near $8. The unit sales average near 1 million, with a standard deviation of 100,000.

The net income averages $20.7 million in this experiment, not far from the $20 in the test in Chapter 5. The results of each experiment should agree if the trials were repeated or if the sample size were increased. However, the standard deviation of net income rose from $8.7 million to $10.8, an increase of approximately 25 percent.

A plot of unit sales and sales price shows why the correlation makes net income more volatile. The trials with the highest sales volume typically occur when the company gets the highest sales price. Likewise, the lowest unit sales tend to occur when sales prices are also low. The correlation measures the tendency for pricing news to reinforce unit sales results.

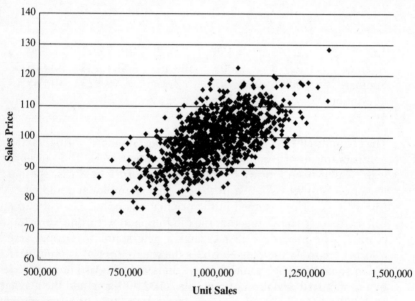

FIGURE Q.4 Sales Price versus Unit Sales

5.7 Create two correlated normally distributed random numbers. The first series represents Project 1 and has a mean of 300,000 and a standard deviation of 250,000. Project 2 has a mean of 500,000 and a standard deviation of 500,000. The correlation between the two series is .4. Add the values together and measure the mean and standard deviation of the sum. Are the sample results roughly consistent with the theoretical mean and standard deviation determined in Questions 2.5–2.8?

Answer:

The table that follows generates two sets of standard normal random variables. Next, use Equation 5.3 to create the column for Project 1 with a mean of 300,000 and a standard deviation of 250,000. Then use Equation 5.4 to combine the two sets of random numbers to produce a correlated series with a mean of 500,000 and a standard deviation of 500,000.

$$X_1 = \text{Mean}_1 + SD_1 * N_1$$

$$X_2 = \text{Mean}_2 + SD_2 * \left(N_1 * \text{Corr} + N_2 * \sqrt{1 - \text{Corr}^2} \right)$$

	N_1	N_2	X_1	X_2	$X_1 + X_2$
	0.766	−0.474	491,557	436,012	927,569
	0.063	1.627	315,747	1,258,185	1,573,932
	−0864	0.871	84,117	726,626	810,743
	.	.	.	.	.
	.	.	.	.	.
	.	.	.	.	.
	−0.065	0.745	283,754	828,373	1,112,128
	−1.035	0.014	41,292	299,253	340,545
Mean	−0.029	−0.057	292,720	467,844	760,564
Standard deviation	1.000	1.000	247,385	506,436	653,706

The results derived from this simulation are consistent with the theoretical mean and standard deviation calculated in Question 2.8. The mean of X_1 is 292,720, close to the expected mean of 300,000. The mean of X_2 is 467,844, which is close to the expected mean of 500,000. The standard deviation of X_1 is 247,385, close to the expected standard deviation of 250,000. The standard deviation of X_2 is 506,436, close to the expected standard deviation of 500,000.

The standard deviation of the sum of X_1 and X_2 is lower than the sum of the standard deviation of X_1 and the standard deviation of X_2.

The standard deviation of the sum exactly matches the level predicted by Equation 2.12.

CHAPTER 6

6.1 Calculate the Black-Scholes call value from the information provided in Question 5.5.
Answer:
The first step is to calculate d_1 and d_2.

$$d_1 = \frac{LN\left(\dfrac{Spot}{Strike}\right) + \left(Rate + \dfrac{\sigma^2}{2}\right) * Time}{\sigma\sqrt{Time}}$$

The formula for d_1 in Excel would look like the following cell formula.

$$= (LN(100/100) + ((5\% + 15\% * 15\%/2) * 1))/15\%/(1^\wedge 0.5)$$

The value for d_1 equals .408.

$$d_2 = d_1 - \sigma\sqrt{Time}$$

The formula for d_2 in Excel would look like the following cell formula:

$$= .408 - 15\% * (1^\wedge 0.5)$$

The value for d_2 equals .258.

Next, calculate the probability for d_1 and d_2 using the cumulative normal distribution. The NORMSDIST function in Excel can calculate this probability:
For $N(d_1)$,

$$= NORMSDIST(.408)$$

The value for $N(d_1)$ is 0.658.
For $N(d_2)$,

$$= NORMSDIST(.258)$$

The value for $N(d_2)$ is 0.602.

Finally, apply the Black-Scholes call option formula.

$$c = \text{Spot} * N(d_1) - \text{Strike} * N(d_2) * e^{-\text{Rate}*\text{Time}}$$

$$c = 100 * 0.658 - 100 * .602 * .951 = 8.592$$

If the sample size is increased, the Monte Carlo can be adjusted to get results consistent with the Black-Scholes call option model.

About the Author

Stuart McCrary is a principal at Chicago Partners, a subsidiary of Navigant Consulting, Inc. Chicago Partners is an economic consulting company involved with forensic accounting, business valuation, securities valuation, labor, anti-trust, and other economic issues. Mr. McCrary is also involved with business valuation, securities valuation, and securities market practices.

Mr. McCrary teaches finance and accounting in the Masters in Product Design Program, an executive masters program in Northwestern University's Robert R. McCormick School of Engineering and Applied Science. He has also taught classes on hedge fund management and alternative investments at DePaul University's Charles H. Kellstadt Graduate School of Business as well as classes in options and financial engineering at the Illinois Institute of Technology.

Mr. McCrary graduated from Northwestern University's Kellogg School of Management with a master's degree in Business Administration and from Northwestern University's Judd A. and Marjorie Weinberg School of Arts and Sciences with a bachelor of arts degree.

Index